PERI

PHRASES

FOR

COACHES

**Hundreds of Ready-to-Use Winning Phrases
for Any Sport—On and Off the Field**

RALPH PIM

McGraw
Hill

New York   Chicago   San Francisco   Lisbon   London   Madrid   Mexico City
Milan   New Delhi   San Juan   Seoul   Singapore   Sydney   Toronto

The *McGraw·Hill* Companies

Library of Congress Cataloging-in-Publication Data

Pim, Ralph L.
    Perfect phrases for coaches : hundreds of ready-to-use winning phrases for any
sport—on and off the field / by Ralph L. Pim.
        p.   cm.
    Includes index.
    ISBN 978-0-07-162857-0 (alk. paper)
    1. Coaching (Athletics)—Terminology.   2. Coach-athlete
relationships.   I. Title.

GV711.P56   2010
796.07'7—dc22   2009013536

1 2 3 4 5 6 7 8 9 10 11 12 13 14 15 16 17 18 19 20 21 22   FGR/FGR   0 9

ISBN   978-0-07-162857-0
MHID   0-07-162857-6

McGraw-Hill books are available at special quantity discounts to use as premiums and
sales promotions or for use in corporate training programs. To contact a representative,
please e-mail us at bulksales@mcgraw-hill.com.

This book is printed on acid-free paper.

To the members, past and present, of the competitive sports team in the Department of Physical Education at the United States Military Academy for their commitment, enthusiasm, professionalism, loyalty, and selfless dedication to the competitive sports vision and mission. Through your passion and perseverance, we are changing the culture of sport one day at a time.

Colonel Gregory Daniels
Colonel Jesse Germain
Lieutenant Colonel Hector Morales
Lieutenant Colonel Joe Doty
Mr. Craig Yunker
Major Khanh Diep
Major Shawn Bault
Major Scott Blanchard
Captain Russ Nowels
Mr. Paul Gannon
Major Joe Gelineau
Major Ken Wanless
Mr. Sandy Helfgott

Contents

Contents

Contents

Introduction

Outstanding coaches select powerful words that inspire and motivate players. They communicate their vision so others want to follow and make it a reality. They define, model, shape, and reinforce team play every day. They develop fundamentally sound players and teams of significance.

Communication is not what you say as much as what your players hear you say. There is a powerful relationship between the words that you use and the results that you get. Highly successful coaches select words that create a visual of the desired outcome. They understand that poorly chosen words hinder team unity, damage self-esteem, hold back enthusiasm, and hurt team morale. Well-chosen words encourage, motivate, energize, and synergize team members.

Never underestimate the power of communication. You may know the technical aspects of your sport and recognize the principles of teamwork, but if you cannot communicate them effectively, your knowledge is of little value. Fortunately for all of us, communication is a skill that we can continually develop throughout our careers.

Perfect Phrases for Coaches was written to help coaches at all levels improve their communication and be the catalysts to develop athletes of character and build winning teams of significance. It is my belief that impact words capture the attention of players and create perfect phrases. This book identifies impact words for each letter of the alphabet that can be incorporated into almost every aspect of coaching. Examples of phrases are then provided for each impact word.

It is my hope that readers will be able to reinforce their coaching philosophy and incorporate these impact words into their talks with their players and assistant coaches before, during, or after a game, during practice, and in individual and team meetings.

Chapter 1

The Definition of Success

Our first stop is to examine the definition of success. Many people do not truly understand the meaning of success. They believe success means playing sports on the professional level, winning championships, obtaining financial security, or making an all-star team. Nothing could be further from the truth. Success should not be measured by national recognition or financial rewards. True success begins with focusing all of your resources on becoming the best that you can be. It comes from knowing that you have given your best effort. Successful players strive to realize their potential.

Hall of Fame basketball coach John Wooden said, "Success is peace of mind which is a direct result of self-satisfaction in knowing you did your best to become the best that you are capable of becoming."

The Wooden-coached UCLA teams reached unprecedented heights that will be difficult for any team to match. The Bruins set all-time records with four perfect 30–0 seasons, 88 consecutive victories, and 10 NCAA national championships, including seven in a row.

Jim Tressel, head football coach at Ohio State University, studied the teachings of Wooden and added one powerful idea to Wooden's definition of success. Tressel expanded the definition to read, "Success is the inner satisfaction and peace of mind that comes from knowing I did the best I was capable of doing for the group." The addition of the words "for the group" helped Ohio State players define success in terms of what the team needs. With the rise of individualism in sports, the concept of being part of a team eludes many of today's players.

Chapter 2

The Path to Success

There are many obstacles that stand between athletes and success. Every day athletes make decisions that ultimately determine whether they will reach their goals. This chapter examines some of the qualities that are necessary to help them overcome these challenges.

Key Traits of Successful Performers

Why are certain athletes able to reach their goals, while others do not? My experiences have shown that successful performers possess five key traits.

1. **Self-respect.** Successful athletes value themselves as important and worthwhile. They hold themselves in high esteem, demonstrate respect for themselves, and take pride in everything they do.

2. **Self-responsibility.** Successful athletes take responsibility for their actions and their attitudes. They set goals and realize they must pay the price for success. They do not blame others for setbacks and are able to stay positive in difficult situations.

3. **Self-confidence.** Successful athletes believe in themselves. They do not allow anything or anyone to diminish their self-worth. They look forward to competition because it is an opportunity for growth. They always give their best effort and trust in the results.

4. **Self-improvement.** Successful athletes continually improve. They strive to master the skills necessary for success. They realize that athletic success is similar to climbing a never-ending staircase. There is always room for improvement, and each new step presents new challenges.

5. **Self-forgiveness.** Successful athletes are able to forgive themselves when they do not live up to their expectations. They understand they will experience setbacks and disappointments in their quest for success. They know how to get back up after they fall.

The Four Cs of Peak Performance

Dr. Ralph Vernacchia, sport psychologist at Western Washington University, believed peak performers combine the personal attributes of attitude, passion, and character with the physical, mental, and emotional characteristics of confidence, commitment, concentration, and composure. Vernacchia branded these characteristics the four Cs of peak performance.

1. **Confidence.** Peak performers are confident, approach competition with positive anticipation, and do not worry needlessly about their ability to perform. They have inner peace in knowing they have prepared themselves for competition and will always give their maximum effort.

2. **Commitment.** Peak performers are relentless in their drive and determination to be the best that they can be. They hold themselves responsible for their actions and do not make excuses. They establish a reputation for giving 100 percent every time they go on the playing field or court.

3. **Concentration.** Peak performers are focused on the task at hand. They attend to the details of their performance and are able to quickly refocus when they get distracted.

4. **Composure.** Peak performers stayed composed. They recognize potential threats to their overall performance and utilize strategies to refocus and perform at the highest level.

Take Control

Successful performers focus on the things within their control. The two most important things that athletes control are their attitude and work ethic.

Attitude

An athlete's success depends on his or her attitude. Peak performers are optimistic and focus on the positive rather than dwelling on the negative. Help your athletes discover the importance of finding something positive in every situation. A positive attitude is the key to happiness in life.

Work Ethic

Don't allow your athletes to settle for anything less than their best effort. Many people do not reach their goals because they do not extend themselves. Successful performers exhibit a tremendous work ethic. They understand there are no shortcuts to success—it takes hours and hours of hard work.

The Complete Player

In addition to the qualities already described, for players to be complete they must fully meet their responsibilities to the team. Doing so requires the traits of unselfishness and perseverance, which, when demonstrated, will not only make their efforts better serve their teammates, but will also set an example for others to follow.

Unselfishness

Teamwork is essential in most sports. Everyone must work together and get along in order to be successful. This does not mean that players have to be best friends with all of their teammates. But it does mean that they have to be willing to make sacrifices and fit within the structure of the team by playing a specific role. It is an athlete's responsibility to learn, accept, and play the role that will best help the team. It is amazing what a team can accomplish if no one cares who gets the credit. Selfishness will destroy a team.

Perseverance

Athletic success does not happen overnight. Every player encounters setbacks throughout the course of a season or a career. Successful athletes have the ability to rebound quickly from mistakes and disappointments. They do not worry about things they cannot control. Once the play or game is over, they move on to the next challenge. They have the ability to stay positive and maintain their motivation during difficult times. An athlete's true test is how he or she handles adversity. Winners are survivors—they find a way to achieve success.

Self-Image

The mental picture a person has of himself is called his self-image. A landmark finding during the twentieth century was the discovery of the self-image as a predictor of human behavior. A person's self-image sets boundaries for accomplishments and defines what he or she can and can't do. If athletes think they are not good players, they won't be. Winners see themselves as successful long before success actually happens because they have a positive self-image. Athletes cannot consistently perform in a manner that contradicts their self-image. Their self-image will either lead them to the top or keep them from fulfilling their dream. There is no factor more important in life than the way people think about themselves. Many of the key phrases featured in this book aim to channel a coach's goals for both team and players in such a way that athletes will incorporate the message into their self-image. Each of the concepts featured in this chapter, along with several others, will play a role as well, ultimately defining what it means to be successful in the process.

Chapter 3

Quality Practice

Improving an athlete's skills requires hours of practice. Many times the difference between becoming a good player and becoming a great player is *how* an athlete practices. Every practice session provides an opportunity for individual and team improvement. It is a coach's responsibility to plan and conduct practices that make the most of this opportunity.

Principles of Practice

To accelerate an athlete's growth as a player, adhere to the following principles of practice:

- **Practice with a purpose.** Plan your practice time wisely. Decide in advance what to do, how to do it, and when to do it. Select drills and activities that will help your team improve. Write down daily goals for practice sessions.

- **Practice makes permanent.** Successful performers maximize their growth because they practice the fundamentals correctly. Pay attention to detail and have your players master the fundamental skills of the game.
- **Practice hard.** There is no substitute for hard work. Successful athletes are dedicated to becoming excellent players and push themselves to reach the next level.
- **Practice smart.** Design practice sessions so you are preparing your team for competition. Going through drills at half speed does not prepare them for live game situations. Your team must practice as if it were a game. Do not waste time practicing skills that your players will never use in a game.

The Three Ps of Quality Practice

Practice sessions should be considered laboratories for learning. To aid in the development of your players, always adhere to the three Ps of quality practice.

- **Be precise.** Successful athletes are precise in the execution of the fundamentals. Hold them accountable to the highest standard, and do not let them take shortcuts.
- **Be present.** Successful athletes stay in the present moment. They do not let past mistakes affect their game. They see the present and concern themselves only with those things they can control at that time.

- **Be patient.** Successful athletes realize that patience is a virtue. Good things take time, and there are many setbacks on the road to success. They believe that good things happen as a result of hard work.

Repetition Is Essential

An athlete's execution on game night depends primarily upon conditioned automatic reflex responses. Players must practice a skill correctly again and again until it becomes automatic. Repetition is the best way to learn a skill so that it becomes a reaction at the instant an athlete needs it.

Incorporate Rest into Your Practice Schedule

Quality rest is essential for peak performance. Rest restores an athlete's energy and must be included in your practice schedule. Allow recovery time for your athletes.

Practice Phrases

Many of the phrases and concepts in the pages that follow will apply to both practice and game settings. It's up to you as a coach to decide when the lessons of each will have the greatest effect. Just as you practice plays and drills so your athletes can refer back to them during key moments, so can you build upon the values imparted using the concepts in this book.

Chapter 4

Characteristics of an Effective Coach

Great coaches identify opportunities for success and empower players to win. Coaches come in all sizes and shapes, but there are ten common characteristics of an effective coach.

An effective coach must demonstrate the following:

1. **Be trustworthy.** Integrity underlies everything that is done in the coaching profession. It is the foundation of how you act as a human being, a coach, and a member of society. It builds trust between you and your players. A lapse in integrity will destroy team unity.

2. **Be knowledgeable and competent.** Coaches should be students of the game and learn everything they can about how to do their job well. This includes understanding the laws of learning, the keys to team building, and the power of positive thinking and being

technically and tactically proficient. Players look to their coaches for answers and solutions, and successful coaches produce positive results.

3. **Be passionate.** Nothing can take the place of passion in a leader's life. When leaders are passionate, it generates enthusiasm. Enthusiasm is paramount for success. A team can never reach its full potential without passion and enthusiasm.

4. **Be a team builder.** Effective leaders create a work culture that promotes team play and collective responsibility. Coach John Wooden told his players, "When you come to practice, you cease to exist as an individual. You're part of a team."

5. **Demonstrate personal courage and mental toughness.** Successful leaders make courageous decisions. "The ultimate measure of a man is not where he stands in moments of comfort and convenience," stated Martin Luther King Jr., "but where he stands at times of challenge and controversy."

   Through the years, many coaches have displayed courage and mental toughness by standing up for what they believed was right, regardless of the consequences. They held on to their strong convictions and beliefs with fierce determination.

6. **Be a communicator.** The ability to communicate is probably the most important skill that a coach can possess, and it consists in many forms: speaking, listening, reading, and writing. A key component of

communication that is often overlooked is active listening. It is important for coaches to realize that there is a difference between hearing and listening. "Most players only hear," said Hall of Fame basketball coach Bob Knight. "The key is listening to what you're being told, what's being said, what is expected of you in your role as part of a team."

Nonverbal messages are an essential component of communication in the coaching process. Coaches must be aware of nonverbal behaviors such as facial expressions, eye contact, gestures, and posture.

7.   **Be a teacher and motivator.** The best coaches are exceptional teachers and motivators. They define, model, shape, and reinforce team play every day. Unselfish teams evolve over time through careful planning and nurturing. "Knowledge alone is not enough to get desired results," said John Wooden. "You must have the more elusive ability to teach and to motivate. This defines a leader; if you can't teach and you can't motivate, you can't lead."

8.   **Be compassionate.** Successful coaches demonstrate personal concern for and interest in the people who work for them. Never underestimate the positive effects that compassion has on your team. Remember the adage, "People don't care how much you know, until they know how much you care."

9.   **Be competitive.** Outstanding leaders are committed to excellence and never accept anything less than the

best effort. They are intensely competitive and are not afraid to take risks. Pat Summitt, the all-time college basketball leader in wins, said, "It's my experience that people rise to the level of their own expectations and of the competition they seek out. Only by learning to compete can you discover just how much you are capable of achieving. Competitiveness is what separates achievers from the average. Too many people elect to be average, out of timidity. They are afraid to make a mistake, or to fail, or to be wrong. They are afraid to find out what's inside of them."

10. **Focus on the most important tasks.** Successful coaches have the ability to focus on what's important and do not get distracted by lesser issues. Legendary football coach Lou Holtz used the acronym WIN to illustrate this point. The letters stood for "what's important now." Weak leaders spend too much time consumed with jobs that are not essential.

In the pages that follow, you'll find not only phrases and maxims intended to help you communicate key ideas and values to your players, but also reminders on what you as a coach need to do to uphold those principles. Not every aspect of coaching can be summed up in a single phrase, but by keeping these tips in mind you'll find that your best method of communication is in your actions and what they represent to the young men and women you are leading.

Chapter 5

Perfect Phrases for Players

Many coaches are faced with never-ending demands on their time and energy. Besides practices to plan and game plans to develop, coaches are expected to educate players on their team's vision and mission, inform parents on their coaching philosophy and organizational structure, address the media, interact with referees, and speak at social gatherings and banquets. Most coaches do not have the time to prepare dynamic and effective presentations for all these occasions.

In the next six chapters, you will be provided samples of model phrases that can be used in many of the specific situations that you will encounter as a coach. These phrases can be easily adapted, perhaps with little more than a change of a word, to meet your particular circumstance.

Coaches interact with individual players almost daily. During individual conversations or meetings, it is important for coaches to use verbal communication as a tool to improve player-coach relationships. Relationships are built on trust and respect. As a coach, be very clear in your intent and ask questions to ensure that the player understands your message. Listen carefully to what the athlete is saying, and also be very conscious of the player's body language. Many times it is difficult for an athlete to feel comfortable expressing his or her thoughts with a coach. This section gives examples of how a coach may discuss a variety of topics with individual players during the course of a season.

Cutting a Player from the Team

After observing and evaluating you during our tryouts, we will not be able to have you continue practicing with our team. We were pleased with your attitude and work ethic, and this is a real credit to who you are. Unfortunately, you lack the [size and quickness] necessary to be a contributor on our team this year.

We truly appreciate your efforts during the tryouts, and we hope you continue your efforts to become the best player that you can be.

If you are truly committed to earning a spot on this team in the future, we can help you develop a program in the areas that you need to improve.

You should consider playing in recreational or AAU programs where you can continue to compete and improve. Another possibility for you this year is to con-

sider becoming part of our program as a team statistician or manager.

We hope that you will be a strong supporter of our team this year.

If we can be of any help to you, we will be happy to do whatever we can.

Code of Conduct for Players

This talk is designed to alert you to the behavior expected of you and to the potential consequences that your behavior may have on your status as a student-athlete. All student-athletes are members of our student body, and all school policies governing student conduct apply to you. Your participation in interscholastic athletics is governed by the rules set forth in our school's Student-Athlete Handbook. These rules are designed to complement the rules that our team has established.

There are two types of misconduct that may affect your ability to participate in our interscholastic athletic program. The first, called Type I, includes violation of a criminal law that is classified as a felony. The second, Type II, includes violation of a school policy or an athletic department policy.

As a student-athlete, if your conduct is in question, you will receive notification of the charges and the evidence against you. You will have the opportunity to explain the circumstances of the situation and refute the charges. If you are found guilty, you will have an opportunity to appeal the decision.

Asking a Player for Clarification About Possible Misconduct

[John], being a member of our team is a privilege. We are very selective as to who gets the opportunity to wear our uniform, and we take great pride in having one of the top athletic programs in the state.

[John], do you have a clear understanding of our team's core values and your responsibilities as a team member to live up to these standards?

It has been called to my attention that your behavior was not conducive to the standards of our program. Have you read the written report of the charges that are being brought against you?

I have a copy of the written report with me. I want you to take as long as necessary to review the report.

After reading the report, are the charges accurate? Please start at the beginning and explain the course of events that occurred on that night.

I have also been provided with the evidence that our authorities have. If you believe that this report and evidence are not accurate, you have the right to refute the allegations against you.

Are you clear on your rights?

Suspending a Player

[John], you and I have had several discussions about the incident that you were involved in last weekend. Based on the facts regarding the incident, a decision has been made regarding your status on our team. As of today, you are suspended indefinitely from our team.

You will no longer practice or compete with our team. This decision was made by our director of athletics and me.

You will receive a written notice of your suspension from our director of athletics. This letter will also include a complete description of the appeal procedures available to you. Part of your suspension requires you to participate in a mentoring program. Our coaches sincerely care about you and want to help you grow both as a student and a future leader.

I want you to carefully read the written notice of your suspension and meet with me again tomorrow so we can begin the mentoring program.

Crossing the Line of Commitment

An important concept on our team is called the line of commitment. There is a piece of tape on the floor outside the door to our gymnasium that every player crosses on his [her] way into practice. This piece of tape represents our line of commitment.

Practice begins the moment that you walk across the line onto the court. When you cross the line, you have declared that you are physically and mentally ready for practice.

It symbolizes your dedication and commitment to our team goals and sets the tone for practice.

Respecting Referees

A key word in our program is respect. Respect is treating people the way they should be treated. If you are respectful, you recognize the dignity and worth of all individuals. Today, I want to talk about respecting referees.

[Robert], have you ever refereed a game?

Were you 100 percent correct in every call that you made?

Did you ever have parents or players treat you poorly when you were officiating?

My point is that officiating is a very difficult job. Most referees are fair-minded people, but they are human and they will make mistakes. Let's put it in this context. It is no more likely that a referee will make all calls correctly than it is that you will make every free throw that you attempt.

It is your responsibility to play the game, not officiate. Do not let a bad call affect you. Keep your mouth shut and keep playing. Stay in the present and focus only on the next play.

Any discussions with referees will come from the coaches, not the players. Being rude or argumentative with referees will not be tolerated. Period. Always demonstrate respect for referees and address them as sir or ma'am.

[Robert], do you have any questions regarding our expectations when it comes to your interaction with referees?

Helping Players Understand Their Roles

As we prepare for our first game, it is essential that every player on our team understand her [his] role.

[Sylvia], you have done a very good job in practice, and the coaches are pleased. You worked hard and competed strongly for a starting position. Striving to earn a starting job is at the very core of individual and team improvement.

As it currently stands, you will not be a starter, but you have earned a position in the playing group. This means that you will help our team succeed by being one of the first players coming in off the bench. The amount of time that you play will depend on many factors such as the strengths and weaknesses of our opponent, the score and time remaining in the game, personal fouls, and the flow of the game.

In practice, we expect you to continue to do your best to earn a starting position. Your effort will not only help you, but it will also help your teammate playing ahead of you. This type of effort is a hallmark of a true team player.

On game night, you must discipline yourself to study our opponent and be prepared to make an impact when you go into the game. Being able to cheer for a teammate who has the starting position that you desire is perhaps the ultimate test of being a selfless teammate.

If you find yourself rooting against the player ahead of you, this is the act of a selfish and immature player, and it will hurt both your progress and our team.

The key to teamwork is to learn a role, accept that role, and become excellent in the role you are assigned. Make it your masterpiece and take pride in the role that you play. Remember, you don't get to move to another role until you have mastered the one that you are in now.

Do you have any questions?

[Sylvia], can we count on you to accept and play this role to the best of your ability?

Academic Progress

[Jason], congratulations on earning a B on your marketing exam. According to the midterm grades, you now have a C in the course. What are you doing to make sure that you continue to improve your grade?

When is the next assignment due?

What do you like most about the class?

Are you still considering marketing as a possible major for you?

[Jason], is there anything that the coaching staff can do to help you?

Academic Deficiency

[Pat], your midterm grades show that you are deficient in English and algebra. We know that you understand the importance of academics. You have also told us that you are working very hard in these classes. But we are disappointed that your grades do not reflect your commitment. Have you talked with your instructors?

What suggestions do they have?

What is your plan to improve your grades?

[Pat], do you need a tutor?

I would like a weekly update on your improvement. Let's schedule a meeting every Friday to discuss your progress.

Missing Class and Lack of Academic Effort

[Barry], your lack of effort in the classroom is totally unacceptable and will not be tolerated. When you fail in the classroom, you also fail in [basketball]. They work hand in hand.

You can't be successful on the [court] if you are failing in the classroom. Over the past week you missed two classes. Your instructors have informed us that you make no effort to be part of class and sometimes fall asleep.

For the next two weeks, you no longer have the privilege to play in our games. You will sit on the bench, dressed in street clothes. You will continue practicing with our team. You will attend a mandatory study hall six days a week. At the end of two weeks, we will reassess your status.

I will be contacting your family today and will explain my decision to them.

[Barry], the ball is in your court now. Either you start taking your academics seriously or you will be dismissed from our team.

Do you have any questions?

End-of-Season Meeting

Today begins the first of several meetings that we will have during the next month. The purpose of today's meeting is to discuss your strengths and identify improvement areas regarding our team's core values.

Next week, we will discuss your offensive and defensive strengths and weaknesses.

One of our team's core values is responsibility. How would you assess yourself in this area? Using a scale from 1 to 5 (1 meaning "never" and 5 signifying "always"), select a number that best represents your actions as compared to the following statements.

- I willingly accept responsibility.
- I do not make excuses.
- I attempt to exceed standards rather than do the minimum.
- I confront teammates who violate team policies rather than look the other way.

Several weeks ago, you were given a self-assessment form. Did you complete the form and bring it with you today?

What core value do you believe that you need the most improvement in?

Let's begin our discussion with that particular core value.

Chapter 6

Perfect Phrases for Teams

Coaches interact with their teams in many different locations. It may occur in the locker room, in a classroom, on the practice floor, on a bus, or in a team huddle. During these meetings, coaches use verbal communication to enhance learning, generate motivation, improve team unity, and present important information. Keep your talks concise and be careful not to give your players so much information that you lose their attention. This section includes a variety of topics that coaches will discuss during the course of a season.

Tryouts

Very shortly, we will be taking the court [field] to begin our tryouts. During tryouts, you will be evaluated in many different areas. These include things such as attitude, character, work ethic, unselfishness, ability, and potential. It is our intent to select the players who will help us become the best team that we possibly can be. We have very high standards for this program. For the returning veterans, we expect more than what you were able to give last year. For the new players, this will be an eye-opening experience. You will be pushed harder than you ever have been.

Our program is built on core values of character, competency, commitment, and cohesion. During the tryouts we will be looking for unselfish, disciplined players who possess these qualities.

Quite frankly, some of you are not going to make it. If we decide that you are no longer a candidate for this team, we will tell you face-to-face.

Listen carefully and adhere to the guidelines for our tryout sessions.

- *Stop immediately when you hear a whistle.*
- *Give eye contact to the coach who is speaking.*
- *Listen carefully to the instructions.*
- *Run from one drill to the next.*
- *Never stop hustling.*
- *Use no profanity.*
- *Be enthusiastic.*
- *Compliment teammates.*
- *Work hard every second you are on the court [field].*

Are there any questions?

Keys for Success

Congratulations, you are now a member of a team that has the opportunity to accomplish great things. Whether this happens is up to each of you. You hold the key that will unlock the energy that this team needs to succeed. Today, we will discuss three keys for success in our program.

The first key is to work hard every day. It is essential to know up front that you will be challenged. We will demand that you always give 100 percent in everything that you do. Practices will be intense and very competitive. We will never settle for anything less than your best effort. There is a direct correlation between a team's record and its work ethic, and our work ethic separates us from everyone else. No opponent will ever outwork us. No opponent will be more committed.

The second key for our team is to have a positive attitude. There is nothing more important than your attitude. The difference between winning and losing is often dictated by a team's attitude. Your attitude will allow this team to accomplish extraordinary things. Attitude is a choice, and bad attitudes are not an option in this program. We will help you maintain a positive attitude at all times.

The third key for this team is unselfishness. Now that you have earned a spot on the team, your goal should be to help improve the team in every way possible. No team will succeed without teamwork, no matter how many all-stars it has. You will always be expected to put the team ahead of any personal feelings, ambitions, and agendas. Teamwork is a form of trust, and it is important for you to realize that your personal goals and the goals of our team are one and the same. We are all in this together through the good times and the bad times.

The coaching staff is excited about the upcoming season. There is tremendous anticipation and optimism. Whether this optimism turns into reality depends on your ability to believe.

Belief is at the core of everything we do in this program. First, you must believe in our program. We will face no opponent that is better prepared. There will be no other team on our schedule that deserves victory more than we do.

Second, you must believe in your teammates. Together we will achieve great things, but it all begins with trust and respect. Trust and respect must be earned. Your behavior should exemplify honesty and trustworthiness. You should demonstrate respect for others at all times. Great teams develop strong bonds among team members. They do not allow teammates to fail.

Third, you must believe in yourself. Belief in yourself occurs when you know that you have done the things that are necessary for you and your teammates to suc-

ceed. It is based on your preparation. No one will believe in you unless you believe in yourself.

In closing, our team will become great because of your work ethic, positive attitude, and unselfishness. Never stop believing in our team or in yourself. Together we have the power to make this a season that we will always remember.

Team Rules

Being a member of our program carries with it certain responsibilities and expectations. You are a highly visible representative of our program and our school everywhere you go. We expect you to carry yourself with class and present a positive image at all times. As a member of our student body, it is your responsibility to adhere to the rules and policies set forth in our school's Student Handbook.

We have one overarching rule for our team. Do not get involved with anything that will bring embarrassment to yourself, your family, our school, or our team.

Specific in-season rules or regulations will be delivered by the coaching staff after consultation with the team captains. We believe each of you should have input regarding our team rules.

Practice Guidelines

These are the practice guidelines expected of every member of our team:

- *Be on time.*
- *Be dressed, on the court [field], and ready to compete prior to the start of practice.*
- *Do not complain or criticize others during practice.*
- *Compliment teammates.*
- *Do not debate with a coach on the court [field].*
- *Give the coaches your undivided attention.*
- *Maintain eye contact with the person who is speaking.*
- *Stop immediately when you hear a whistle.*
- *Move quickly to get into position to start a new drill.*
- *Never stop hustling.*
- *Do not use profanity.*
- *Be enthusiastic.*
- *Every practice is designed to improve team play, team unity, and individual play.*

Preparing a Team with a Losing Record for Postseason Play

At the end of every season, the reset button is pushed and all teams start with a clean slate. The wins and losses from the season are erased, and everyone's record goes back to 0–0. The teams that succeed in postseason tournaments are the ones that still have their dreams. They have learned from their mistakes and refuse to let their winning spirit and positive attitude be extinguished. They know that it is not always the team with the most talented players that wins a championship. It is the team that has players who work best together. This tournament gives us the opportunity to demonstrate who we really are.

Let's make sure that we understand some basic facts:

- *No team in the tournament has more heart than we do.*
- *No team has improved more than we have.*
- *No team has learned how to maximize its strength better than ours has.*
- *Our focus is on playing hard, playing smart, and playing together.*

We will divide the game into five-minute segments and find ways to succeed during each period. We will reduce unforced turnovers and create high-percentage scoring opportunities.

We will be tenacious on defense and limit our opponent to one shot. We will take pride in everything that we do. We will never be outworked.

Preparing a Team with a Winning Record for Postseason Play

There is incredible excitement as we enter postseason play. Week after week, we met the challenge of the regular season. Everyone feels good about the accomplishments of our team. Our fans are talking about us advancing to the state tournament. But it is time for a reality check.

Today, every team in the state has a record of 0–0. Every win and every loss has been erased. Every team has new life. Every team can make its season by beating us.

It is time for us to focus on the most important phase of our season, and that is postseason tournament play. Remember that it is not where you start, it's where you finish that matters.

Our preparation and attention to detail will determine our success. There are three keys. First and foremost, focus on one game at a time and one play at a time. In tournament play, the margin for error is extremely small. One missed defensive assignment, one turnover, or one bad shot can mean the difference between advancing to the next round or going home.

Second, put away your press clippings and stay away from people who are looking ahead to the next round and telling you how great you are.

Third, get your rest and maintain the mind-set of a warrior. Focus on what must be done on the playing court rather than on the hype of the tournament.

Our team has all the ingredients necessary for success in postseason tournaments. These are defense, depth, and experience. Respect every opponent but be confident in our abilities. Enjoy the journey, and let's make it happen one day at a time.

Pregame Talk Prior to a Championship Game

Every practice and every game has prepared us for tonight, and now the championship is ours for the taking. We have worked harder than any team in America. We know the endless hours, the commitment, and the courage it took to keep on trying when everything within us was telling us to quit.

Tonight, we will succeed because we have worked harder, practiced longer, and sacrificed more.

- *We have had a great week of practice.*
- *We understand the keys to victory.*
- *We have poise and confidence, and deservedly so.*

What I want is for each of you to be prepared for the unexpected. Read the situation and make the necessary adjustment. The outcome of this game will be determined by our execution and heart.

This is our night. This is our game. And this is our championship. Let's go out and get it!

Postgame Talk After a Win

Good job tonight. We got excellent support from our bench. We had outstanding teamwork and communication on offense. We accomplished many of our objectives. But there is one key area that must be improved in order for us to continue our winning streak. This vital area is defense.

Never forget that defense wins championships.

Tonight we lacked the aggressiveness to create turnovers. We did not have active hands or quick feet. We did not get loose balls due to poor anticipation. These are all areas that we can improve.

Enjoy the victory, but come to practice tomorrow ready to take the next big step.

Postgame Talk After a Loss

Keep your heads up and listen very carefully. Tonight, we suffered a very difficult loss. Our desire to win was there, but we did not execute and perform at the level that was necessary to earn a victory.

When faced with a setback such as this, we have two choices. We can make excuses why we lost, or we can intensify our emotions and find ways to overcome the challenge. There is no question in my mind as to what choice this team will make. It is these moments that determine our destiny.

Losses on the scoreboard are simply outcomes that we must learn from. It is our responsibility to recognize what went wrong and then take the appropriate action. All of us must work harder and learn from our mistakes so we don't have another performance like tonight.

Come to practice tomorrow with positive energy and be mentally prepared to take the next step.

On a Losing Streak

Unfortunately, many fans classify teams into two categories. They are either winners or losers. Do not listen to those people who look at our record and want to call us losers. Losers are people who have given up, and there is no one in this locker room who will ever give up. Keep the faith and never stop believing in each other.

It is during difficult times that players learn the importance of being a team member.

- *Reach out and help your teammates.*
- *Never feel sorry for yourself.*
- *No one will ever break our spirit or take away our desire to win.*
- *We will never back down from an opponent.*
- *We will find strength in adversity and take action to improve.*

Come to practice tomorrow with positive energy and be mentally prepared to take the next step.

On a Winning Streak

We are undefeated and have won [10] games in a row. Sportswriters and fans are singing our praises and calling us a great team. They are mistaken. We are not a great team at this point.

We have a long way to go before the word great *can be used with our team.*

Never take winning for granted. Never start feeling too good about what we have achieved so far this year. Our focus must be on getting better every day. Teams become great because their players are totally committed to do whatever it takes to reach their goals.

We will be persistent in our drive to become champions. We will not let up. We will maintain our hunger to succeed. We will outwork every opponent and never back down.

Put your sense of importance on hold and keep your ego in check. The championship ring will go to the team that is relentless in its pursuit of success.

Rebuilding a Program

There is no quick fix to turning around this program. It will take many small steps to get us to the top, and we cannot skip steps. It starts with a crystal clear vision of where we are going.

For everyone in this room, our vision is to establish the premier program in the state.

We will have the most committed and hardest-working athletes. Our athletes will bond together into a single, selfless unit and accomplish memorable feats through their commitment to excellence. Our athletes will combine mental toughness, perseverance, and athletic skills with exemplary sportsmanship and fair play. They will have a teachable spirit and demonstrate the drive, will, and courage to stay committed and succeed regardless of the challenge.

Our program will be built on core values that establish the foundation for everything that we do. The core values for our team are integrity, respect, responsibility, unselfishness, courage, and tenacity. We will break down our core values into teachable parts both on and off the playing field. These behaviors will set the standard for our program, and it is every player's responsibility to live up to the standard.

Each of you must clean your emotional house and get rid of negative baggage. Let go of any issues that you have had in the past and focus on the present.

- *Come to practice eager to learn, and be open to constructive criticism.*
- *Admit mistakes and learn from them.*

- *Place the team ahead of personal goals and individual statistics.*
- *Be willing to play any role in order to make our team successful.*
- *Stay fully committed to our team's mission.*
- *Refuse to allow your spirit to be broken.*
- *Never make excuses.*
- *Always show respect for your teammates.*
- *Hold yourself and your teammates accountable.*

Step by step, our dream will become reality, so never stop believing in it. Always demonstrate the courage to do the things that it will take for us to become the premier program in the state.

Chapter 7

Perfect Phrases for Parents

No matter what age level you coach, it is very helpful to develop good working relationships with your athletes' parents. They should have the opportunity to become acquainted with you and understand your coaching philosophy and program objectives. It also helps when parents know your team rules, regulations, and operating procedures. In many cases, parents become your greatest allies and will reinforce the standards you have established for your team.

There may be parents who do not know much about your sport. Providing explanations and demonstrations could help them gain a greater appreciation of what their child is experiencing. They should also be aware of potential risks in your sport so they can make informed decisions regarding their child's participation.

You may encounter parents who have been influenced by the professional sport model and overemphasize winning at the expense of fair play and sportsmanship. There are also parents who are more concerned with attracting college scholarships than just enjoying their child's athletic experiences. These parents often spend large sums of money for high-exposure camps, individual tutors, and conditioning coaches. Their main focus is on spotlighting the talents of their child, and they have little regard for anyone else.

The key to working with different types of parents is direct communication. Many problems can be avoided by having an open line of communication with your parents. Make sure they have an opportunity to hear your coaching philosophy, team rules, player expectations, parent expectations, practice times, and game schedules. Parents should also have an opportunity to ask questions and express their thoughts. Coaches use many different types of settings to become acquainted with their parents. A few examples are monthly booster club meetings, a parent orientation program, postgame picnics, fund-raising events, and team breakfasts.

Always be well prepared and organized when meeting with your parents. The following section has key points and phrases that can be used in discussions with parents regarding the good and bad sides of sports, coaching philosophy, winning with honor, building a team of significance, fair play and sportsmanship, qualities of a successful athlete, and the role of parents on game day.

The Good Side of Sports

Many important lessons can be learned through participation in athletics when coaches develop value-based sport programs. Today we are going to talk about the good side of sports and give examples of some of the lessons that can be taught in athletics.

- *Sports can teach athletes about fair play and sportsmanship.*
- *Sports can teach athletes about teamwork and help them become better team members.*
- *Sports can provide athletes with an opportunity to focus on something bigger than themselves.*
- *Sports can help athletes develop a strong work ethic.*
- *Sports can provide athletes with the moral courage to stand up for what is right, especially when it is not easy or popular.*
- *Sports can teach athletes about human diversity.*
- *Sports can help athletes learn how to build trust with teammates.*
- *Sports can teach athletes the importance of preparation.*
- *Sports can improve athletes' self-discipline and self-control.*
- *Sports can teach athletes to face adversity.*

- *Sports can help athletes learn how to focus amidst distractions and pressure.*
- *Sports can teach athletes how to win and lose with dignity.*
- *Sports can help athletes learn how to set goals and have the perseverance to reach them.*
- *Sports can teach athletes how to listen and follow directions.*
- *Sports can help athletes develop mental and physical toughness.*

The Bad Side of Sports

We truly believe in the good side of sports, but as parents and coaches, we must be aware there is also a bad side of sports. We feel it is necessary to mention some of the possible negative outcomes of sport participation.

- *Sports can give athletes a false sense of self-importance and promote selfish behavior.*
- *Sports can teach athletes that it is acceptable to cheat as long as they do not get caught.*
- *Sports can allow talented athletes to act like arrogant bullies.*
- *Sports can permit star athletes to take shortcuts and neglect their academic development.*
- *Sports can create a sense of entitlement for athletes.*

- *Sports can lead athletes to irresponsible behaviors such as taking harmful supplements or illegal drugs.*
- *Sports can hurt an athlete's self-esteem.*
- *Sports can lead to unhealthy levels of stress for athletes.*
- *Sports can produce parents who overvalue athletic achievement and are negative role models.*

Let's make sure that we are working together to help your son [daughter] have the type of experiences that can positively influence his [her] personal growth.

Your Coaching Philosophy

The purpose of sport is to provide experiences that teach lessons that transfer into life-enhancing skills and qualities such as character, courage, desire, dedication, commitment, perseverance, selfless service, teamwork, and self-discipline. Your son [daughter] is participating in a program designed to develop athletes of character and build teams of significance.

Let's first look at the definition of an athlete of character. An athlete of character is a team player who combines mental toughness, perseverance, and athletic skill with exemplary sportsmanship, fair play, and integrity. An athlete of character has a teachable spirit and dem-

onstrates the drive, determination, and courage to stay committed and succeed regardless of the challenge. Through sport, an athlete of character learns how to compete honorably.

Now let's look at the definition of a team of significance. A team of significance comprises a group of athletes who bond together into a single, selfless unit and accomplish memorable feats through their commitment to excellence. Six essential components for a team of significance are character, courage, competency, commitment, communication, and cohesion.

It is important that all our players understand the definition of success. Success is the peace of mind that you have when you have done everything possible to become the best that you can be. There is no mention in our definition that an athlete has to earn all-state honors or a team has to win on the scoreboard in order to be considered successful. A player can be successful and not be in the starting lineup. A team can be successful and still score fewer points than its opponent. The true measure of winning is preparing young people for success in today's world.

Winning with Honor

Let me start by saying that winning is important in sport. If it weren't important, we wouldn't have scoreboards. We also know that society judges coaches on their winning percentage. *There have been many outstanding teachers and coaches who have lost their jobs only on their win-loss record. Society clearly rewards winners. Unfortunately, too much emphasis is placed on the final outcome.*

Coaches have to resist the forces that encourage them to win at all costs. Winning should never occur at the expense of the total development of an athlete. To win by cheating is not really winning at all.

Your child is participating in a program that teaches athletes how to win the right way. We refer to this as winning with honor. Learning how to win is one of the greatest lessons learned through athletic participation, as long as athletes are taught how to win the right way. Your son [daughter] will very seldom hear us say the word winning. We prefer to talk about the performance goals that must be met in order for us to win.

We tell our players the specific things that must be done for us to win. For example, your son [daughter] might be instructed to block out his [her] opponent on every possession. This provides clear instructions to a player rather than just saying, "Go out and win."

Make no mistake about it: our players have the desire to win and possess the dedication to prepare to win. This is reflected in what we call the winning spirit. Our practices are designed to teach the winning spirit. Players are taught to give their best effort no matter what the score or situation. Quitting is never an option. We take great pride in knowing that no matter what the scoreboard reads, no opponent will ever take away our winning spirit.

In athletics, it is unrealistic to believe that athletes will never experience losing. Losses hurt, but they must be viewed as opportunities to learn and improve. Losing forces players and coaches to analyze why the loss occurred and make the necessary adjustments so mistakes are not repeated. Losing can create a drive and determination to work harder. Most athletes appreciate success even more after experiencing losing. When faced with losing, players and coaches can develop the resilience and mental toughness needed to keep bouncing back from disappointments. Players in our program are taught how to lose with dignity. Poor sportsmanship and inappropriate conduct such as temper tantrums are not tolerated. We teach our athletes how to recover from a loss. It is essential that they maintain their winning spirit and diligently prepare and focus on the next challenge. It is not a time to doubt their abilities or lose confidence in our team.

Building a Team of Significance

Your child is participating in a value-based sports program. The purpose of the program is to develop athletes of character who bond together to form a team of significance. In an earlier meeting, I discussed our coaching philosophy and defined an athlete of character and a team of significance.

As a quick review, an athlete of character is a team player who combines mental toughness, perseverance, and athletic skill with exemplary sportsmanship, fair play, and integrity. This athlete has a teachable spirit and demonstrates the drive, determination, and courage to stay committed and succeed regardless of the challenge.

A team of significance comprises a group of athletes who bond together into a single, selfless unit and accomplish memorable feats through their commitment to excellence. Six essential components for a team of significance are character, courage, competency, commitment, communication, and cohesion. We follow a four-step method to develop a team of significance:

- *Step 1. We establish core values. Our core values are the heart and soul of our team and become the indispensable and lasting tenets of our program. They become the glue that holds our team together during the good times and the bad times.*
- *Step 2. We define our core values in behavioral expectations. This will bridge the gap between words and actions by describing the expected behavior for each of our core values. Our core values now become our team's code of behavior. Our players learn what is and what*

isn't acceptable. The ultimate goal is for our core values to become the moral compass for decision making.

- ***Step 3.*** *The coaches teach the appropriate behaviors for our core values in every aspect of our program. We break down our core values into teachable parts both on and off the playing field. These behaviors set the standard for our program, and it is every player's responsibility to live up to the standard.*
- ***Step 4.*** *We practice and model our core values in everything that we do. This also means correcting a teammate when he [she] is not acting appropriately. Through positive peer pressure, players hold each other accountable to the standard.*

The core values for our team are integrity, respect, responsibility, unselfishness, courage, and tenacity.

Our first core value is integrity. Integrity is the cornerstone of good character and encompasses every part of your life. Players with integrity do not lie, steal, cheat, or intentionally deceive others.

Our second core value is respect. Respect is treating people the way they should be treated. If you are respectful, you recognize the dignity and worth of all individuals.

Our third core value is responsibility. When you are responsible, you are dependable and reliable and all team members can count on you.

Our fourth core value is unselfishness. Unselfishness is putting the needs of the team ahead of your own.

Our fifth core value is courage. Courage is having the conviction to do what is right, regardless of the circumstances.

Our sixth core value is tenacity. Tenacity refers to the mental and physical toughness of every team member. Tenacious players relish competition and do not shy away from physical contact. They take pride in knowing an opponent will never outwork them.

In closing, thank you for your support of our program. It is a privilege to work with your sons [daughters], and it is our intent to help every athlete learn valuable lessons that will prepare him [her] for success in life.

Fair Play and Sportsmanship

Two of the most important components of our value-based program are fair play and sportsmanship. It is important for all of us to know that sport does not teach character. It reveals character. We believe it is our responsibility as coaches to teach character through sport.

Athletics provide a great venue for participants to learn the importance of fair play and sportsmanship. The media often highlight athletes, coaches, and parents portraying poor sportsmanship. Fortunately, there is more emphasis on fair play and sportsmanship than even a decade ago. National associations, conferences, and individual schools are promoting fair play and sportsmanship.

Programs are in place to recognize schools and individual athletes who demonstrate these qualities.

Team guidelines are in place that promote these values:

- *Profanity and vulgar language will not be permitted.*
- *Temper outbursts after a mistake, loss, or poor performance will not be tolerated.*
- *Over-celebration and taunting will not be permitted.*

We want all our players to become athletes of character, and we need your support to ensure this happens. We discuss fair play and sportsmanship and clearly define what acceptable behavior looks like.

We also define what unacceptable behavior looks like. On some teams, illegal acts are even encouraged and taught, and their coaches give the impression that it is not cheating unless you are caught.

On our team, your son [daughter] will be taught how to play within the rules and the spirit of the game. Your son [daughter] will not cheat or use gamesmanship tactics to gain an unfair advantage. Your son [daughter] will be taught how to show respect for referees and opposing players. Your son [daughter] will congratulate opponents following either a victory or a loss. Your son [daughter] will be taught how to maintain self-control when others are acting poorly.

Qualities of a Successful Athlete

There are 10 qualities that we believe separate successful athletes from unsuccessful athletes. As parents and coaches, it is important for us to work together to help your son [daughter] develop the following traits:

- *Sportsmanship and fair play*
- *An unselfish commitment to teamwork*
- *The will to win*
- *A desire to learn and improve*
- *Self-discipline*
- *Self-respect*
- *Self-control*
- *The hard work and willpower to achieve goals*
- *The ability to focus and perform under pressure*
- *The resilience and perseverance to rebound from defeat*

The Role of Parents on Game Day

As a parent, you play a vital role in helping your children understand the true meaning of sport. We hope that you will actively support our program's value-based objectives. We want your child to learn valuable life lessons through his [her] participation in our program. Help us make this a positive experience for the athletes.

- *Encourage fair play.*
- *Demonstrate good sportsmanship.*
- *Applaud teamwork and hustle.*
- *Keep your emotions under control.*

Accept the judgment of the referees without criticizing. When you outwardly criticize a referee, it sends a message to the players that it is acceptable to challenge authority.

Please don't try to coach your son or daughter during the game. Players should have only one voice giving them advice. We do not want your message, as a parent, and our message, as coaches, to conflict. Players should be focused on the game rather than looking at their parents.

Try to view the game with team goals in mind rather than focusing on the number of points that your son or daughter has scored. Be a source of encouragement to all of our players.

Reward effort and teamwork rather than centering your attention on the final score. Always remember that the single most important thing that you can do for your son or daughter is to model appropriate behavior. Demonstrate winning and losing with dignity.

After the game, keep your corrections and criticisms in check. It may be best to give your son or daughter space and time after a game if it is needed. Wait to ask questions or give your opinions until your son or daughter wants to talk about the game.

Let's work together to make each game a positive learning experience for everyone involved.

Chapter 8

Perfect Phrases for the Media

Many coaches have opportunities to speak with members of the media, and it is vital to develop good working relationships with the press. Here are some key points when working with the media. Treat members of the press with respect and always strive to generate positive public relations for your school and your team. Know who you are talking with and the media outlet that he or she represents. Listen to the reporter's entire question, and if the question is unclear, ask him or her to repeat or clarify it. Always think about your answer before speaking. Be brief and to the point. Remember, everything you do or say may appear in print or be broadcast.

Scouting Report of a Ranked Team

[State] is one of our longtime rivals, and we always look forward to this game. Without question, [State] is one of the top teams in the country. It is well coached, and it is deep in talent. [State] rebounds and runs the fast break better than any team we have faced this season. It can beat you in many different ways.

There are two keys for us. First, we must block out and not allow [State] to get second and third shot attempts. Second, we must sprint back on defense and eliminate fast-break points.

Defensively, [State] puts tremendous pressure on the ball handler. The players do a great job of making opponents play a tempo that they are not used to. This often results in turnovers and fast-break points.

Offensively, we have to reduce our number of unforced turnovers. Whenever we play [State], you can throw out the records. It's always a hard-fought game.

Postgame Talk After a Loss to a Ranked Team

[State] is a very, very good team. It deserves its high ranking. We had a game plan that we felt good about, but [State] kept us from executing it. We played hard, but we were not able to match up with the [State] players' size, speed, and quickness.

We have to learn how to compete at a higher level against an outstanding team, such as [State], for a longer period of time. We had to play almost a perfect game in regard to eliminating mental mistakes, and we just didn't do it. We had several scoring droughts during the second half, and [State] capitalized on our inability to score. We have to learn from our mistakes and continue to get better because our schedule does not get any easier.

Postgame Talk After a Hard-Fought Loss

We are very proud of our team. We played with great intensity the entire game. We competed every minute of the game. We never backed down. We played with a warrior's mind-set.

This loss is difficult to take because we played well enough to win. Our players must look at the positives. We fought hard the entire game and almost pulled off a major upset.

This game can give us the momentum to finish the season strong.

Postgame Talk After a Blowout Loss

First and foremost, [Central] stormed out of the gate and took the game right to us. The players did an excellent job of exploiting our weaknesses. [Central's] pressure forced turnovers and quick shots. The players beat us down the floor and created high scoring opportunities. [Central] has a great defense, and it is a real struggle to score points against them.

When you don't execute the fundamentals against a talented opponent, the result most often is a blowout loss. We have to learn how to start games better. We cannot fall behind as much as we did tonight, because it makes it very difficult to come back.

We never stopped fighting, but we must learn how to protect the ball. One of the purest forms of toughness is to be strong with the ball. We didn't show that tonight. We must improve in this area in order to be a good team.

Postgame Talk After a Close Win

We played a very good team today, and the opponents brought out the best in us. We were challenged to get this victory.

[South] is disciplined, the players play hard, and they are well coached. We beat a high-quality opponent. This win was very important for us and will give us confidence going into our next game. Our players did an excellent job during the closing minutes of the game to secure the victory.

We will be in a lot of close games this year, and it is essential that we learn how to win these types of games. Our team members played with a lot of heart, and I'm really proud of them.

Postgame Talk After Snapping a Losing Streak

This has been a difficult time for us. Our schedule has been very demanding, and we got knocked down a few times because we were not playing strong defensively.

This was a very important game for us. We had to find a way to recover, and this was a big step in the right direction. An important key for us tonight was to reestablish our defensive mind-set. We had lost our defensive intensity the past few games, and that is the backbone of our team. Tonight we wanted to regain that defensive edge.

We worked hard in practice on pressuring the ball handler and keeping the ball out of the middle. We are very pleased with the results. Defense is a mind-set, and we must maintain our defensive focus.

Thanking the Fans for Their Attendance and Support

We really appreciate the fan support that we received tonight. The fans brought tremendous energy. They really helped us get the game started the way we wanted to play. The fans were great the entire game. The crowd was awesome, and our team fed off their support.

Chapter 9

Perfect Phrases for Banquets

Coaches will have opportunities to speak at many different types of banquets. Two of the most common are award ceremonies and alumni gatherings. At the conclusion of a season, most teams hold a banquet for parents, players, and friends. During this special event, coaches recognize and honor their athletes and thank their supporters. Many schools also have alumni banquets to unite and recognize former student-athletes. The key to making a powerful presentation at a banquet is to personalize your comments so they are meaningful to the recipients.

Coaches should prepare for public speaking appearances the same way they prepare for games. They should determine ahead of time what they want the audience to gain from their speech. Their thoughts should be organized so there is a natural flow from one topic to the next. Spontaneous comments rarely work well, so it is advisable to write out the script beforehand. Public speakers should always be conscious of the time factor and plan accordingly. A common problem with banquets is that they become too lengthy.

Be careful when attempting to use humor in your speech. Unless you are an experienced public speaker and possess a natural, universal sense of humor, it is probably best to avoid it. You should also stay away from telling inside jokes, because most of the audience will not understand what you are saying. Always consider beforehand how a remark will be perceived—especially by the parents. Avoid sarcasm and negativity. Make only positive comments about players.

The following sections have sample speeches that can be used at banquets celebrating either a winning or losing season, as well as phrases that are appropriate for an alumni function.

Speech After a Winning Season

Let's start by acknowledging something that we all know: it's good to win. Our season has ended, and our record is now in the books for everyone to remember. But there is another factor that means more to me than anything else. And that is, we won the right way.

Our record serves as an outstanding tribute to the desire, dedication, and determination of a very special group of athletes. It reflects countless hours on the practice fields. It represents hard work, commitment, and self-discipline.

Our record also serves as a reminder that success must be earned and nothing comes without paying the price.

Our team stayed together during the good times and the challenging times. Our players persevered through several heartbreaking losses and rebounded stronger than ever. Our players stayed committed from start to finish. They never lost their focus on our team goals. They never stopped believing in each other, and they possessed the courage to never let anyone or anything take away our dream. This team will always hold a special place in my heart. Their winning spirit, competitiveness, and togetherness will serve as the standard for future teams.

Tonight, we must also look at our record and see in it something else. Yes, our team members were vitally important. But there was another group that was just as necessary to the total victory. I am speaking of you— our parents, our loyal fans from the community, and our students. Your support was second to none both at home and on the road. You were with us in the joy of victory, and you had faith in us when things looked bad. You lifted our spirits and strengthened our desire to succeed. You gave every ounce of your energy to make this season a success. This is your record also. We couldn't have done it without you.

It was a magnificent year. It started as a dream and culminated with the [conference championship]. We applaud your dedication, your winning spirit, your sacrifice for the good of others, and your willingness to work together for a common goal. We believed, we prepared, we competed, we persevered, and we succeeded. Thanks to each of you for the role that you played in this championship season.

Speech After a Losing Season

This dinner tonight stands as a testimony to how everyone feels about this special group of athletes. It provides an opportunity to look back at our successes over the past season.

At first, you may question my use of the word successes to describe the events of this past year. If a team's record is nothing more than a number indicating the games won and lost, then I suppose we would have to agree that this season was not the best in our school's history. But I believe that a team's record stands for a lot more than what is indicated in the win-loss column.

When I look at the team record, I ask myself the following questions:

- *Did the team become the best that it could be?*
- *Did the players stay united throughout the entire season?*
- *Did the team compete every minute on the playing field and refuse to ever quit?*
- *Did the players demonstrate respect, responsibility, integrity, sportsmanship, fair play, and unselfishness?*

If the answer to all of these questions is yes, I would call that team successful. And that is definitely the case with the team we are about to honor.

- *Our team was committed and dedicated the entire season.*
- *They refused to be outworked no matter what the situation.*
- *Our players were united and never stopped believing in each other.*
- *Our players never backed down from a challenge or quit.*
- *They demonstrated the strength and courage to pick themselves up after many heartbreaking losses.*
- *They allowed nothing to defeat their winning spirit.*
- *Our team's optimism never faltered.*

This group of athletes should be a source of pride for everyone associated with our school. They demonstrated to all of us what commitment really looks like. Our seniors learned valuable lessons that will help them be successful throughout their lives. Our returning players established a strong foundation that will pay dividends next year. The experiences of this season have prepared us to take the next step.

To our fans, we thank you for your unwavering support. You lifted our spirits and strengthened our desire to succeed. You never stopped believing in us.

We are all very proud of these players and excited to honor them this evening.

Speech to an Alumni Gathering

I am delighted to see each and every one of you, and I am honored that you invited me to speak with you tonight. This evening has sparked memories from years gone by when our relationships were a bit different than they are now. Back in those days, I had a whistle around my neck and you wore skimpy shorts that today's players laugh at. For many of us, our hair was a lot longer and our waistlines a lot smaller.

Who will ever forget our preseason conditioning programs or the infamous "blood and guts" drill?

Who will ever forget putting on the varsity uniform for the first time? That uniform represented pride, belief, trust, and togetherness.

Who will ever forget our games with our archrival [Central] and the joy of hard-earned victories but also the anguish of heartbreaking defeats?

I have so many memories, but if you asked me to say what I remember most clearly and with the greatest affection, I would have to say it is your passion. You were passionate about our sport, passionate about our team, passionate about our school, passionate about each other, and passionate about life.

As I spoke to you earlier this evening, I was thrilled to find that the intervening years have not lessened your passion for life.

Of course, our roles and our priorities have changed, and that is inevitable. Today you are concerned with the future of your families and providing them with opportunities for rich and rewarding lives. You hold jobs where you influence and impact others. Yet what made you special as student-athletes has not changed through the years. The qualities of honesty, hard work, perseverance, courage, and passion are still the driving forces in your lives.

Through the years, many of you have thanked me, but it really should be me thanking you for the opportunity that I had to be in your lives. My heart is filled with joy as I see all of you today.

Thank you again for asking me to be here tonight, and may your future always be as happy as my memories of you in the past.

Closing Speech After a Fund-Raising Drive

It is an honor to be able to start this speech with three magnificent words. You did it! You reached your goal. You have worked for something in which you all believed, and because of your common effort, that goal has been reached.

This is indeed a time to celebrate, but it is also a time to pause, reflect, and be thankful for the power of teamwork. We have before us a prime example of what can be done when people believe and unite for a common goal. For years to come, your efforts will be an example of selfless dedication. Thousands of student-athletes will reap the benefits from your hard work and generosity.

You have my utmost respect for a job well done. Thank you for your commitment and your dedication. Now it is time for all of us to enjoy the festivities of the evening.

Chapter 10

Perfect Phrases
for Inspiration

Most coaches entered the coaching profession because they were influenced by a teacher or coach who inspired them to achieve and accomplish things that may have seemed too difficult or impossible at the time. Inspiration is a powerful force when it is used for noble and wholesome purposes.

There are three key components when giving inspirational talks. First, you must consider your target audience and gauge if the timing and subject matter is right for this type of talk. Second, you must be sincere and really believe in what you are saying. And third, you must exhibit passion and enthusiasm.

In this section you will find a variety of topics, situations, and phrases that can be used in your inspirational talks for players and general audiences.

The Acronym PRIDE

Pride is the result of being and doing your best. The acronym PRIDE can be your backbone for success.
The letter P stands for passion.

- *Passion is at the heart of most successes.*
- *Passion results in positive energy.*
- *Passion generates enthusiasm.*
- *Passion can be seen in the work ethic and attitude of a champion.*
- *Passion provides the motivation and drive to persevere in difficult times.*
- *A team can never reach its full potential without passion.*

The letter R stands for respect.

- *Respect is essential for building team unity.*
- *A player with respect accepts the differences among team members.*
- *Respect is treating people the way they should be treated.*
- *A respectful person recognizes the dignity and worth of all individuals.*
- *Respect your teammates and coaches.*
- *Respect referees and opponents.*

- *Respect yourself.*
- *Respect the game.*

The letter I stands for integrity.

- *Integrity is the cornerstone of good character.*
- *A person with integrity does not lie, cheat, or steal.*
- *If you have integrity, your words are free from deceit and your actions are consistent with your words.*
- *Integrity means doing the right thing.*
- *The most important asset that a person has is his or her integrity.*

The letter D stands for desire.

- *Champions have the desire to succeed.*
- *They never let anything keep them from their dreams.*
- *A player with desire will do whatever it takes to be successful.*
- *Success begins with the burning desire to succeed.*

The letter E stands for enthusiasm.

- *Nothing great was ever achieved without enthusiasm.*
- *Never underestimate the power of enthusiasm.*

- Enthusiasm is contagious.
- Create enthusiasm and energy in everything you do for our team.

Tenacity Is Our Trademark

Tenacity is the trademark for our team. It refers to the mental and physical toughness of every team member. When you are tenacious, you dive for loose balls and take charges. You sacrifice your body for the good of the team.

Tenacious players relish competition and do not shy away from physical contact. Tenacious players thrive in competitive situations. They perform their best during crucial moments in a game. They overcome all challenges and keep fighting regardless of the conditions. They possess the discipline and inner drive to give their best regardless of the score, weather, or any condition that may be a distracter.

One of the best ways to measure tenacity is by watching players during the entire course of a game. Does the score or the amount of time remaining in a game affect the players' attitudes and intensity levels? Tenacious players make the maximum effort every minute of every game. They never quit. This one component separates great players from good players.

A spectator walking into an arena after the start of a game should not be able to tell from the intensity level *whether it is a one-point game or a 20-point game. Quitting is never an option for tenacious players. Even when the outcome of the game has been decided, tenacious players play hard until the game is over.*

As coaches we never stop coaching. Our teams are always trying to make one more basket or get one more defensive stop. Tenacity in sports transfers into tenacity in everyday living. We are all trying to win in the big game of life, and one of the most important principles is to never give up.

What Are the Core Values of Your Team?

Every person here is currently a member of several different teams. Your family is a team. Your student body is a team. Your athletic department is a team. The athletes in your sport create a team. Today we are going to take the first step toward building a team of significance in your sport. Take the team that you are currently on and ask yourself, "What does my team stand for?"

What would your answer be?

All teams are linked together by something. Hall of Fame basketball coach Pat Riley calls this link a covenant and defines it as an agreement that binds people together. Sometimes a covenant is written and expressed as a team's core values. Oftentimes it is unspoken and is expressed through the actions of the players. The fact is that all teams create covenants simply by being together. Some covenants are better than others. And some can be very destructive.

Many teams end up being unsuccessful because they are built on selfishness and negativity. All of us can probably think back when we were members of a team that was built on negative covenants. A team where players felt it was acceptable to put the team second if they felt slighted or were jealous of others on the team.

Together, let's discuss ways that we can build our team on positive covenants. Before you is a sheet with a list of 25 values. [Coaches can use the values discussed in this book, along with their own, to compose the list.] Without any input from your teammates, review and study the list of values. Circle all of the words that are very important to you. There are a few blank lines at the bottom of the page for you to add any other values that are important to you.

Now, narrow the list to eight values.

Now, narrow the list to six values.

And finally, choose your top four values and rank order each one.

The purpose of this exercise is to help you clarify the values that you believe are essential for your team to become great. It is a much more challenging exercise than you may think at first.

Now, sit down with your teammates and coaches and compare answers. Together, establish the core values for your team. This process of identifying core values is critical to a team's success.

- Core values define a team and provide a unique identity.
- Core values set the standard for behavior and performance.
- Core values serve as the glue that bonds the team together.
- Core values provide a moral compass for decision making.
- Core values become the heart and soul of a team.

The next exercise is to define the behavioral expectation for each core value. Core values must be more than just words. They have to become actions. Describe what you think "right" looks like for each core value. Also describe what you think "right" does not look like.

It is important that all players have a clear understanding of the appropriate behavior for each core value.

The next step is to get players to commit to the core values. Teams that have players who have not committed themselves to the core values are always very fragile. On the surface, everything looks good, but when there is any type of controversy or adversity, the foundation of the team starts to crack. Splinter groups start to form within the team. Players involve other players in their disappointments or anger. Small groups within the team begin to congregate and discuss their problems. When it comes to adherence to core values, there is no in-between. A player is either in or out.

Great teams have players that take ownership of their team's core values. These players demonstrate what right looks like during every part of the team experience, and they hold their teammates accountable for their actions.

Teams that create and embrace their core values become energized, focused, and confident. My desire is that each of you gained valuable information today that will enable you and your teammates to accomplish the goals that you have set for the upcoming year.

Never Lose by Default

You should never lose by default. Too many people today lose by default. They may show up physically, but they don't show up mentally. Many players are defeated before the game ever starts. There is no excuse for this. Every player on this team has the obligation to do the very best that he [she] can at all times. There is no exception. Stop making excuses.

Every [basketball] team in the country is dealt the same number of cards at the beginning of a game: five. Every team has a hand. Some teams have aces, and some teams have deuces. It is our job to play the cards that we are dealt the best that we can. We do this by taking own-

ership of those factors that we can control such as our intensity, our work ethic, our attitude, our tenacity, our competitiveness, and our will to win.

- *It is time for each of you to stand up and be counted.*
- *Mentally prepare yourself to be a warrior athlete of character.*
- *Never allow any opponent to work harder than you do.*
- *Stand toe-to-toe with our opposition.*
- *Never back down.*
- *The heart of a warrior never dies.*
- *Success has a narrow door.*

The Five Cs of Building a Championship Team

There are five essential components when building a championship team.

- ***Character.** There is nothing more important than character. Character makes trust possible, and trust is one of the cornerstones of leadership.*
- ***Competence.** A championship team must have highly talented team players. Team players place the success of the team ahead of individual goals*

and personal glory. Team players trust their teammates and coaches. Team players refuse to let a teammate fail.

- **Commitment.** *The level of team success depends on the team members' commitment to the team's vision and mission.*
- **Cohesion.** *Championship teams develop a strong bond among team members. The players stay united no matter how difficult the circumstances.*
- **Communication.** *Communication is based on trust and respect. Athletes of character always speak the truth when communicating.*

You Can Make the Difference!

Every person on our team plays a vital role in our success. Never underestimate the power of one person. I often hear people ask, "Why should I vote in elections? My vote is only one among thousands." What is one vote? Here are a few examples of the importance of one vote. Thomas Jefferson was elected president by one vote in the Electoral College. So was John Quincy Adams. The War of 1812 was brought on by a series of events based on one vote. The successor to Abraham Lincoln, Andrew Johnson, was saved from impeachment by one vote. We do make a difference, each and every one of us.

Our goal of winning the conference championship is a reality within our grasp. Each of you will make the difference in whether we have a good season or a great season. There are many ways that you will make the difference.

- *It is being devoted to our team's mission and rules.*
- *It is believing in yourself and your teammates.*
- *It is embracing discipline for the benefit of the team.*
- *It is putting the team ahead of yourself in every decision.*
- *It is bringing an unquenchable desire to succeed every day.*
- *It is competing every minute and never giving up.*
- *It is demonstrating the inner strength to persevere and succeed in pressure situations.*
- *It is accepting and fulfilling a role.*

Every day your actions help define our team. Attack this season with an "I will make a difference" attitude, and you will experience the beauty of your dreams.

Chapter 11

Impact Words from A to Z

A

Accountability

"The most important quality that I look for in a player is accountability. You've got to be accountable for who you are. It's too easy to blame things on someone else."

> —*Lenny Wilkens, Hall of Fame basketball player and coach*

- Take full responsibility for your words and actions.
- Hold yourself accountable to a higher standard than others do.
- Excuses and alibis are the main enemies of accountability.
- Players can't become accountable until they understand exactly what is expected.

Actions

"As I grow older, I pay less attention to what men say. I just watch what they do."

> —*Andrew Carnegie, business leader*

- Achievement requires action.
- Don't tell me how good you are, show me!
- Your actions reflect your attitude, not your words or how you say it.
- Do your actions match your words?

Adaptability

"Adapt or die."

—General Douglas MacArthur

- Nothing stays the same.
- Change is inevitable.
- Every day brings its own challenge.
- Be flexible.
- Be willing and able to adapt your behavior and actions as needed.
- Successful athletes quickly recognize their current situation and act in the appropriate manner.

Adversity

"Why do we fear adversity when we know it is the only way to truly get better?"

—John Wooden, Hall of Fame basketball player and coach

- Adversity is inevitable.
- Every team and every player goes through difficult times during the course of a season.

- The real question is not whether you will face adversity, but how you will respond to it when it comes.
- There are two ways that you can deal with adversity. You can close your eyes and hope it goes away, which doesn't accomplish anything. Or you can roll up your sleeves and attack the problem with courage and tenacity.
- Do not let adversity take away your dreams.
- Adversity is part of the journey toward success.
- Look at adversity as a challenge, not a threat.
- Adversity will only make us more determined to reach our goals.
- There is no strength where there is no struggle.
- You will find out more about yourself during times of adversity than during times of celebration and joy.

Anger

"Anger, resentment, envy and self-pity are wasteful reactions . . . [that] sap energy better devoted to productive endeavors."
—*Ruth Bader Ginsburg, U.S. Supreme Court justice*

- Anger is a slippery slope to failure.
- Anger disrupts concentration.
- When you're angry, you can't think, can't focus, and can't control your muscles.
- Being angry is not being prepared.
- Control your emotions.

Athlete of Character

"A warrior athlete of character is a team player who combines mental toughness, perseverance, and athletic skill with exemplary sportsmanship and fair play."

—Ralph L. Pim, educator and athletic administrator

- Honor the game by playing within the rules and the spirit of the game.
- Never cheat or use gamesmanship tactics to gain an unfair advantage.
- Promote character development within the team.
- Correct a teammate who plays unfairly or exhibits inappropriate conduct.
- Show respect for referees and opponents.
- Win or lose with dignity.
- Maintain self-control in response to any physical or verbal harassment.
- Refrain from heckling, trash-talking, and over-celebrating.
- Exhibit the moral courage to compete ethically.
- Demonstrate the discipline and inner drive to give your best regardless of the score, weather, or any other distracter.
- Never quit.
- Display an unwavering commitment to team goals.
- Exhibit a winning spirit.
- Start and finish all endeavors with positive energy and enthusiasm.
- Motivate and inspire teammates.
- Compliment rather than criticize teammates.

- Exemplify team pride both on and off the athletic playing field.
- Show respect for coaches and listen intently to their instructions.
- Admit mistakes and learn from them.
- Exhibit the courage to do the right thing even when others are acting poorly.

Attitude

"The longer I live, the more I realize the impact of attitude on life. Attitude, to me, is more important than the past, than education, than money, than circumstances, than failures, than successes, than what other people think or say or do."

—Charles Swindoll, pastor and author

- Nothing is more important than attitude.
- Great performances start with great attitudes.
- The final outcome of most games is affected more by attitude than by talent.
- More players fail because of poor attitudes than in any other way.
- The foundation of a good attitude consists of thinking positive thoughts.
- A good attitude and a bad attitude are really just two different ways of looking at the same situation.
- Attitudes are like a virus, they're contagious.
- Attitude is a choice.
- You make a choice every day regarding the attitude that you will embrace for that day.

- Take ownership of your attitude.
- Don't let other people or external circumstances affect your attitude.
- Your attitude has a powerful impact on your teammates and affects everything that we do as a team.
- You have an obligation to develop and maintain a positive attitude.
- Our team will have the best attitude in the country.
- Program yourself to have a positive attitude.
- We will not accept bad attitudes.

B

Balance in Life

"I try to keep a balance with all the people and things I love in life. I don't want to be one-dimensional and have my whole life revolve around a series of screens and picks to produce a basket."

—*Mike Krzyzewski, Hall of Fame basketball coach*

What you tell your players about maintaining a balance in life and the battles they choose to fight is just as relevant to you and your career as a coach, so take it to heart.

- Determine your priorities in life.
- Create time for those things that you value.
- Be careful not to become one-dimensional.
- Don't let your goals smother your personal life, your relationships, or your health.

- Work to maintain balance.
- Most attributes can be taken to excess.
- Don't let one aspect of your life consume so much of your time and energy that you neglect the others.
- Don't ignore your family and friends because of your drive, passion, and intensity.
- Always look at the big picture.
- Success will be short-lived if you haven't kept balance in your life.
- Being successful will be empty if you arrive there alone.
- If you lose the balance in your life, you lose in the long run.

Battles

"You don't fight battles over peripheral issues. You fight battles over principles. You don't always want to be drawing the line in the sand."

—Rick Pitino, NCAA champion basketball coach

- Pick your battles wisely.
- Know what is nonnegotiable.
- Never sacrifice your core values.
- Don't get into personal battles.
- Keep your ego and pride in check.
- Don't get caught up with always having to be right and get your way.
- Understand how and when to compromise.
- Don't fight going uphill. Be in the best position to win the battle.

Belief

"If people believe in themselves, it's amazing what they can accomplish."

—Sam Walton, business leader

- The greatest obstacle to success is a lack of belief.
- If you don't believe you can be the best, you'll never give yourself the opportunity to triumph.
- The size of your belief is directly proportional to the size of your success.
- Believing that something is possible makes it possible.
- What you believe, you can achieve.
- No matter how bleak things may appear, never stop believing in yourself.
- Lose your belief and you will lose everything.
- Believe in the power of the team.
- Never stop believing in our team just because the scoreboard indicates we scored fewer points than our opponent.
- If you believe in yourself and your teammates, then we can overcome all challenges.

Body Language

"If an athlete wants to be perceived as a focused and relentless competitor, then he must know how to look the part before he can play it."

—H. A. Dorfman, sport psychologist and author

- Your body language is critical to your success.
- Poor body language leads to poor performance.

- Never project frustration, anger, fear, or anxiety through your body language.
- If you don't feel confident, fake it until you make it.

Burnout

"Burnout in sports is a condition in which the athlete experiences stress over an extended period of time resulting in reduced motivation and interest in the activity. In short, you're worn out, tired of the sport, and don't ever want to see another racket, bat, or helmet again!"

—John Murphy, sport psychologist and author

- The positive traits of desire and commitment can result in burnout if carried too far.
- Too much pressure from within can be frustrating and lead to burnout when the results are not coming.
- Focus on improvement rather than winning.
- Take care of yourself mentally and physically.
- Make sure that you are getting enough rest.
- Everyone has a breaking point.
- Know when to take a step away from your sport.
- Allow time to recover.
- Schedule time away from your sport.

C

Caring

"Two aspects of caring help us succeed: caring about our goals and dreams, and caring about our teammates, without whom we'll never achieve anything."

—Joe Torre, major-league baseball champion manager

- Caring creates team togetherness.
- Exhibit concern and empathy for others.
- Offer support to those teammates who are struggling.
- Coaches must always remember that players do not care how much you know, until they know how much you care.

Challenges

"Accept the challenges, so that you may feel the exhilaration of victory."

—General George Patton

- Life is one challenge after another.
- Our program will challenge you physically and mentally.
- You must meet the challenge to achieve excellence.
- Embrace the challenge. Do not shy away from things that make you uncomfortable.
- Reach out to your teammates during challenging times because nothing will defeat us when we stay united.

Champions

"Champions aren't made in gyms. Champions are made from something they have deep inside them: A desire, a dream, a vision. They have to have last-minute stamina, they have to be a little faster, and they have to have the skill and the will. But the will must be stronger than the skill."

—Muhammad Ali, Hall of Fame boxer

- True champions do whatever it takes to excel.
- The characteristics of a champion are hard work, initiative, vision, and character.

- The fuel that drives champions is caring, conviction, and commitment.
- Champions never complain because they are too busy getting better.
- Champions put themselves in a position to be successful.

Championships

"Talent wins games, but teamwork and intelligence wins championships."

—Michael Jordan, Hall of Fame basketball player

- Individuals play the game, but teams win championships.
- Championships are the by-products of individual hard work and unselfish team play.
- If we are going to be a championship team, we have to think and act like champions.

Character

"Be more concerned with your character than with your reputation. Your character is what you really are, while your reputation is merely what others think you are."

—John Wooden, Hall of Fame basketball player and coach

- Athletic competition does not teach character, it reveals it.
- Coaches teach character.
- As players you must know what acceptable behavior is and what it isn't.
- Character can be learned and improved at almost any age.
- Character is a choice.

- Your character is revealed through your actions.
- The real measure of your character is what you would do if you knew that no one would ever find out.

Chemistry

"The best teams have chemistry. They communicate with each other and they sacrifice personal glory for the common goal."
—*Dave DeBusschere, Hall of Fame basketball player*

- Chemistry is the magic ingredient of a winning team.
- A team's core group has a great impact on team chemistry.
- Athletes who are committed to their team's core values create good team chemistry.
- Teams that have self-centered and unhappy athletes create a chaotic environment.

Remember: Successful coaches do not necessarily play their team's most talented athletes; they play the players who work best together to make a cohesive unit.

Choices

"As simple as it sounds, we all must try to be the best person we can by making the best choices and by making the most of the talents we've been given."
—*Mary Lou Retton, Hall of Fame gymnast*

- Success is a choice.
- You must decide what you want, why you want it, and how you will achieve it.

- Every day you are faced with choices that ultimately decide whether you succeed or not.
- You choose whether to have a positive attitude or a negative attitude.
- You choose whether to go the extra mile and have a second-to-none work ethic.
- You choose whether to put your heart and soul into everything that you do.
- You choose whether to fight through adversity.
- You choose whether to place the team ahead of personal goals.
- Athletes who continually make poor choices continually underperform.
- Always remember that the things that happen to you are a direct result of the choices that you make.
- Your choices will determine our decision whether we want you to be part of this team.

Coaching Profession

"To me, the coaching profession is one of the noblest and most far-reaching in building manhood. No man is too good to be an athletic coach for youth."

—Amos Alonzo Stagg, Hall of Fame football and basketball coach

- Coaching is a profession of value and eternal hope.
- The coaching profession helps shape character, instill values, and develop teams of significance.

- Never take lightly the responsibilities and obligations that come with the coaching profession.
- The coaching profession provides coaches the opportunity to teach athletes the fundamental building blocks to success in life.

Comfort Zone

"Those athletes who aspire to excellence in their mental game are willing to sacrifice 'comfort' and ease."
> —H. A. Dorfman, sports psychologist and author

- Comfort zones enhance laziness and restrict innovation and energy.
- It takes courage to leave your comfort zone.
- Our program will take you out of your comfort zone.
- You will gradually be pushed to new levels of success.

Commitment

"There are only two options regarding commitment. You're either in or you're out. There's no such thing as life in-between."
> —Pat Riley, Hall of Fame basketball coach

- Commit to excellence. Do everything to the best of your ability.
- Life takes on a new significance when you commit to excellence.
- Commitment separates dreamers from achievers.
- Teams succeed based on teammates' commitment to one another and the team.
- Goals set without commitment are wasted.

- Your rewards in life will be in direct proportion to your commitment to excellence.
- Being committed is doing whatever it takes to be successful (assuming that your actions are legal, ethical, and moral).
- How committed are you to the success of our team?
- Do you live each day devoted to our team's mission and rules?
- Do you always put the team ahead of individual goals?
- Do you bring an unquenchable desire to succeed every day?
- Do you compete every minute and never quit?
- Are you the first to arrive on the practice floor and the last to leave?
- Do you willingly make the sacrifices that success demands?
- Do you display mental and physical toughness at all times?
- Do you accept responsibility and never make excuses?
- Do you do the right thing even when no one is watching?
- Are you committed to daily improvement?
- Are you committed to being positive and optimistic every day?
- Do you accept your role and fulfill it to the best of your ability?
- Do you recover quickly from mistakes?
- Will you always believe in our team, even if we are not winning?

Communication

"The most important thing in coaching is communication. It's not what you say as much as what they absorb."

—*Red Auerbach, Hall of Fame basketball coach*

- Communication is the key to trust.
- Always speak the truth when communicating.
- Effective teamwork begins with communication.
- Communication must be taught and practiced.
- Listening is the most neglected communication skill.
- Be an active listener.
- We will work on improving our communication every day in practice.
- You are always communicating either verbally or nonverbally.
- Be very conscious of your nonverbal communication.
- Eye-to-eye contact between the speaker and the listener is a requirement for this team.
- One person speaks at a time.
- When a coach or player speaks, there will be no whispering or talking between the team members.
- During a team huddle, all eyes are on the person speaking.
- Every player should feel comfortable communicating within the team.
- If you are unhappy with your playing time or have something you want to communicate, I do not want to hear it from a third party. Come directly to me.

Competition

"The ultimate victory in competition is derived from the inner satisfaction of knowing that you have done your best and that you have gotten the most out of what you had to give."
—*Howard Cosell, journalist and sports commentator*

- Competition is a natural part of life.
- You compete every day of your life.
- It is important that you learn how to compete.
- Competitiveness requires commitment and risk-taking.
- Competitiveness separates good players from average players.
- Competition helps athletes grow and expands their vision of what is possible.
- Competition keeps you focused and makes you work every day to get better.
- Every second of a competition is important.
- Regardless of the score, never stop competing.
- Don't compete to validate your self-worth.
- Compete for the sheer enjoyment of the competition.

Competitor

"A competitor will find a way to win. Competitors take bad breaks and use them to drive themselves just that much harder. Quitters take bad breaks and use them as reasons to give up."

—Nancy Lopez, Hall of Fame golfer

- A competitor demonstrates a commitment to excellence.
- A competitor exhibits confidence based on preparation.
- A competitor competes ethically and demonstrates fair play and sportsmanship at all times.
- A competitor is mentally tough and brings an unquenchable desire to succeed every day.
- A competitor has the personal courage to do the right thing even when no one is watching.

- A competitor takes ownership of the controllable things.
- A competitor lets go of those things that are uncontrollable.
- A competitor is unselfish and places the team ahead of personal goals.
- A competitor maintains focus and concentration on the task at hand.
- A competitor competes every minute.
- A competitor never gives up.
- A competitor lives each day devoted to the team's core values.
- A competitor brings passion and energy to the team every day.
- A competitor feels the need to raise the bar and sets new goals.
- A competitor looks forward to every challenge.
- View your opponents not as threats, but as catalysts that help bring out your best performance.
- True competitors realize the real competition is not their opponent. The real competition lies deep within them.

Complacency

"When a great team loses through complacency, it will constantly search for new and more intricate explanations to explain away defeat."
    —*Pat Riley, Hall of Fame basketball coach*

- Complacency is the enemy of our dreams.
- Never become satisfied with where you are.

- Look around our team and see whether our mind-set is one of ambition and excellence.
- Anytime you lose that drive to be the best, defeat is near.
- Even when we become number one, we must work harder so that we never lose our edge.
- Don't start feeling too good about what you have accomplished because when you are celebrating, an opponent is working hard to knock you off.
- Where there is complacency, mistakes are tolerated and excuses prevail.
- Where there is complacency, there is no sense of purpose.

Concentration

"Concentration is basketball in a nutshell. Concentration leads to anticipation, which leads to recognition, which leads to reaction, which leads to execution."

—Bob Knight, Hall of Fame basketball coach

- Outstanding performance requires outstanding concentration.
- Concentration is a skill and can be learned.
- Concentration is focusing on the things that will make you successful during competition.
- Concentration requires mental discipline.
- When it is time to perform, focus on the task that needs to be done.
- Train your eyes to see what's happening on the court or playing field.
- Train your ears to listen carefully to what is being said.

- Perform in the moment.
- Eliminate distractions.
- Keep everything inside the lines when you compete.
- Don't let outside influences affect you.
- Self-doubt and self-blame interfere with concentration.

Confidence

"Experience tells you what to do; confidence allows you to do it."
—*Stan Smith, Hall of Fame tennis player*

- Confidence is a learned attribute.
- Confidence precedes success.
- Confidence is a state of mind.
- Confidence is contagious.
- Confidence gains trust from others.
- Confidence is built one step at a time.
- Self-confidence is the first step to success.
- Set task-specific goals, and you will build confidence as you achieve each goal.
- Give yourself credit for the ways in which you have improved and grown.
- To succeed, you must think and feel you are better at your sport than your opponent.
- Attack life with enthusiasm and an "I can" attitude.
- You must be tough-minded and not allow criticism to affect your self-confidence.
- Do not give in to your self-doubt.

- The greatest obstacle to confidence is fear of failure.
- Lack of confidence breeds lack of achievement.

Conflict

"I could have conflict in this job every minute of every day. There's a conflict waiting to happen with every one of these players, with my assistant coaches, with the front office, with the media, and with the owners."

> —*Chuck Daly, Hall of Fame basketball coach*

- Conflict is often an everyday occurrence.
- Conflict is not necessarily a bad thing.
- As long as conflict is resolved effectively, it can lead to team growth.
- Team members develop stronger mutual respect and become more united when conflict is resolved effectively.
- If conflict is not resolved, it will destroy team unity.
- Get issues out on the table as soon as possible.
- Deal with problems appropriately.
- Always treat everyone with respect.
- Do not make personal attacks.
- Stay calm.
- Think clearly.
- Listen first; talk second.
- Consider compromise.
- Control your ego.
- Do not let your pride get you into unnecessary conflicts.
- Demonstrate the courage to make the difficult decision.

Consistency

"Realize that consistent performance is the result of consistent behavior, and that consistent behavior requires consistent thought."

—*H. A. Dorfman, sport psychologist and author*

- No team can become a champion by playing brilliantly one game and terribly the next.
- Develop consistency by making your play in practice as gamelike as possible.
- Consistency builds confidence.
- Your teammates want to know that they can count on you day in and day out.
- Don't let yourself get too high or too low after wins and losses.
- Consistency is developed through constant repetition of thoughts and movements.
- Establish daily routines based on what it takes to become an outstanding performer.
- Trust your routines.

Control

"He who controls others may be powerful, but he who has mastered himself is mightier still."

—*Confucius, philosopher*

- Take ownership of the things in your life that you can control.
- Let go of the things that you cannot control.

- Two important areas that you control are your work ethic and your attitude.
- To worry about things beyond your control is counterproductive and wasted energy.

Core Values

"What I have learned as a head coach is that there are certain values that a player must have to be successful in our program and we must never deviate from these values."
—*Tom Crean, NCAA basketball coach*

- Core values are the heart and soul of a team.
- Core values become the indispensable and lasting tenets of a program.
- Core values define a team.
- Core values set the standard for behavior and performance.
- Core values become a team's code of behavior.
- Core values give team members a standard to live by.
- Core values serve as the glue that binds players together during both the good times and the challenging times.
- Core values provide a moral compass for decision making.

Courage

"To see what is right and not do it is a lack of courage."
—*Confucius, philosopher*

- Courage is a learned quality.
- Courage is contagious.

- Courage enables you to bring out the best in yourself and your teammates.
- Courage is having the conviction to do what is right, regardless of the circumstances.
- Courage means daring to do what you dream.
- Have the courage to do the actions that are necessary for our team to succeed.
- Each time we confront fear we gain courage, because we become more confident that reality is not as bad as the threat.
- Successful athletes have both the ability and the courage to act decisively.

Criticism

"Criticism may not be agreeable, but it is necessary. It fulfills the same function as pain in the human body. It calls attention to an unhealthy state of things."
—*Prime Minister Winston Churchill*

- Our team rule is that we will criticize the performance but not the performer.
- All criticism will be constructive criticism.
- Criticism is intended to inspire learning rather than allocate blame.
- Criticism will be offered at the appropriate time and in an appropriate manner.
- Criticism creates opportunities for improvement.

Critics

"It is not the critic who counts. . . . The credit belongs to the man who is actually in the arena, . . . who strives valiantly; who errs and comes short again and again, . . . who at the best knows in the end the triumph of high achievement, and who at the worst, if he fails, at least fails while daring greatly; so that his place shall never be with those cold and timid souls who neither know victory nor defeat."

—President Theodore Roosevelt

- As players, your performance will be under constant scrutiny.
- As coaches, our decisions will be questioned, criticized, and second-guessed.
- Sometimes it will feel like we are walking around with a bull's-eye on our chests.
- Maintain your composure.
- Don't take criticism personally.
- Resist the temptation to doubt yourself, even when critics do.
- Stay mentally tough when under fire from the media and fans.
- If you worry about what other people are thinking, you will not succeed in athletics.
- If you let the critics determine your self-worth, you will definitely fail.

D

Dedication

"The only thing that counts is your dedication to the game. You run on your own fuel; it comes from within you."
—Paul Brown, Hall of Fame football coach

- Champions dedicate themselves to succeeding.
- When there is a job to be done, you must be willing to put in whatever time it takes to finish it.
- Your dedication will be measured by how close you come to reaching your potential.
- Be the first one on the practice field and the last one to leave.
- Be the hardest worker on the team.
- Be passionately committed to our team's mission.
- Live according to our team's core values.
- Exceed standards rather than do the minimum.

Desire

"The starting point of all achievement is desire. Keep this constantly in mind. Weak desires bring weak results, just as a small amount of fire makes a small amount of heat."
—Napoleon Hill, author

- Success begins with the desire to succeed.
- Champions have an insatiable appetite for being the best.
- If you lack desire, you will always underachieve.
- Upsets occur when the underdog wants victory more than the favorite and is willing to pay the price to make it happen.

- Your desire to succeed is more important than anything else.
- Do you have that burning desire to be the best team player that you can be?

Discipline

"I believe in discipline. You can forgive incompetence. You can forgive lack of ability. But one thing you cannot ever forgive is lack of discipline."

—*Forrest Gregg, Hall of Fame football player*

- Discipline is the trademark of our program.
- It separates us from our competition.
- Discipline is essential to success.
- Disciplined teams always finish strong.
- Discipline makes up for a lack of talent.
- A highly disciplined team often beats a talented team that lacks discipline.
- The goal of discipline is to teach self-discipline.
- Self-discipline is the internal mechanism that drives you to do what is needed in order to be successful.
- Self-disciplined players have a positive effect on everyone around them.

Dreams

"The future belongs to those who believe in the beauty of their dreams."

—*Eleanor Roosevelt, author and civil-rights advocate*

- All great accomplishments start with a dream.
- Dream big.
- Dreams fuel your enthusiasm and passion.
- Surround yourself with people who believe in the dream.
- Chase your dream.
- Hold on to your dream.
- Never allow the skeptics in your life to take away your dream.
- No dream is out of reach for a talented, unselfish, and hardworking team.

E

Ego

"If you want to reach a state of bliss, then go beyond your ego and the internal dialogue. Make a decision to relinquish the need to control, the need to be approved, and the need to judge. Those are the three things the ego is doing all the time. It's very important to be aware of them every time they come up."
—*Deepak Chopra, physician and author*

- Don't let your ego get in the way of your success.
- Remember, the world doesn't revolve around you.
- When you think you are something special, disaster is just around the corner.
- Once your ego takes over, your mind shuts down.
- Check your ego at the door.
- Don't ever think you are irreplaceable. There is always someone who can and will take your place.
- Don't ever feel that you have all the answers.

Energy

"A leader has the vision and conviction that a dream can be achieved. He inspires the power and energy to get it done."
—*Ralph Lauren, fashion designer*

- Bring positive energy to our team every day.
- Don't waste emotional energy on things you can't control.
- Remain positive, energetic, and committed at all times.

Enthusiasm

"Nothing great was ever achieved without enthusiasm."
—*Ralph Waldo Emerson, philosopher and poet*

- To reach your potential, enthusiasm and hard work cannot be separated.
- Enthusiasm without hard work leads to unrealized potential.
- Hard work without enthusiasm leads to boredom.
- Don't ever underestimate the power of enthusiasm and hard work.
- Enthusiastic players energize the team because they are always playing with their hearts.
- Enthusiasm is contagious.
- Create your own enthusiasm every day.
- There are times that you have to fool yourself and show a little more enthusiasm than you feel.
- Your enthusiasm is an indication of how important this team is to you.
- As coaches, we often will know how we are going to do in a game by looking at the sideline and seeing the energy and enthusiasm of our team members.

Excellence

"If you don't seek perfection, you'll never reach excellence."
—Don Shula, Hall of Fame football coach

- There are no shortcuts to excellence.
- Demonstrate the will to excel every day.
- Excellence is the gradual result of always wanting to do better.
- Set and maintain high standards.
- When you lower your standards, you invite mediocrity.

Excessive Emotion

"Winning or losing in the NFL is about execution. It's not about banging your head against a wall or a locker on your way out to the field. That's not what this game is about. That's over by the second play."
—Bill Belichick, NFL champion football coach

- Too much excitement is just as detrimental as too little excitement.
- Excessive emotion makes it difficult to think and react properly.
- Don't let your emotions get the best of you.
- Stay in the "zone" for peak performance.
- Play fast but under control.
- Stay calm and focused.
- Be quick but don't hurry.

- Determine the most effective emotional level for peak performance based on your personality.
- Great performers are able to adjust their ability to either "psych up" or "psych down" based on their feelings during competition.

Excuses

"Blame is the coward's way out."

> —*Elvin Hayes, Hall of Fame basketball player*

- Excuses and alibis are the main enemies of accountability.
- Underachievers make excuses for themselves and blame others for their mistakes.
- Excuses are not an option.
- No one is interested in excuses, only results.
- Don't tell me how difficult it is. Just get the job done.
- Stop wallowing in self-pity.
- We will start winning when we get rid of excuses as to why we can't win.

Execution

"You don't beat people with surprises, you beat them with execution."

> —*John McKay, NCAA champion football coach*

- The purpose of games is to execute and win.
- The success of our team depends on proper execution of the fundamentals.

- The team that normally wins is the one that makes the fewest mistakes.
- If you think that small things don't matter, think of the last game that you lost by one point.

F

Failure

"I have failed over and over again in my life. And that is why I succeed."

—Michael Jordan, Hall of Fame basketball player

- Do not fear failure.
- Every player and every team will experience failure.
- Failure is part of the cycle for success.
- Anticipate that there will be failure on the pathway to greatness.
- Realize that you can handle any loss or failure.
- Learn from your failures and continue on.
- Take away the expectations of others and failure is a lot less scary.
- To anticipate failure is the perfect recipe for failure.
- Failing in a specific situation in a game is not the same as being a failure as a person.

What is the best definition of failure?

- Failure is having goals but not making the commitment to reach them.
- Failure is talking about success but not having the desire to do whatever it takes.

- Failure is being dishonest with yourself and your teammates.
- Failure is quitting and not having the courage to persevere through difficult times.

Faith

"He who has faith has . . . an inward reservoir of courage, hope, confidence, calmness, and assuring trust that all will come out well—even though to the world it may appear to come out most badly. Setbacks will stop us cold if we don't have faith."

—B. C. Forbes, financial journalist and author

- Things rarely go as planned.
- Have faith that hard work and a positive attitude will enable you to get the most out of the situation.
- You must be able to withstand negative events without allowing them to destroy your optimism.
- Keep the faith.
- Never stop believing.
- Never quit working.

Fatigue

"Fatigue makes cowards of us all."

—Vince Lombardi, Hall of Fame football coach

- Great competitors do not give in when they're tired.
- Push yourself to the next level.
- Do not allow fatigue to defeat you.

Fear

"One who fears failure limits his activities. Failure is the opportunity to begin again more intelligently."
—*Henry Ford, business leader*

- Everyone experiences fear.
- It's how you handle fear that will impact your success as a player.
- You can't conquer fear until you recognize it.
- Learn how to confront your fears.
- Look fear right in the eye and defeat it.
- Demystify the concept of failure.
- It begins with an inner battle.
- Dealing with fear is an internal process that ultimately enables you to overcome your anxieties.
- The acronym FEAR stands for "false expectations appearing real."
- The fear of failure is what keeps many people from attempting anything truly outstanding.
- Fear of failure is best fought with preparation, confidence, and discipline.
- You will never reach your potential if you fear failure.
- Overcoming the fear of failure is one of the last hurdles separating a player from greatness.

Feedback

"Feedback is the breakfast of champions."
—*Ken Blanchard, author*

- As coaches, we will give you performance feedback.
- We will let you know where you stand and how to get better.
- If you're doing something we don't like, we will tell you straight out what's wrong and how we expect you to correct it.
- We will look you in the eye and tell you the facts.

Focus

"You must remain focused on your journey to greatness."
                —*Les Brown, entrepreneur and author*

- Learn from the past but focus on the present.
- Keep a laserlike focus on your goals.
- You will reach your goals by focusing on what you want, not on what you don't want.
- Your focus from beginning to end determines the outcome.
- Focus on what you have to do at this moment to excel.
- Never lose sight of what is important.
- Keep the main thing the main thing.
- Focus and finish.
- Take care of the small details, and the big picture will take care of itself.
- Do not let clutter get into your head.
- Eliminate as many distractions as possible.
- Players often lose their focus because of boredom and complacency.
- Focus is a critical part of discipline.

Fundamentals

"Fundamentals and morale are the two most important things in the development of a successful football team."

> —*Amos Alonzo Stagg, Hall of Fame football and basketball coach*

- The foundation of your game must be built on fundamentals.
- Fundamentals are the most crucial part of the game.
- If you are going to be the best, you have to master the fundamentals.
- Repetition, repetition, and repetition is the way to learn fundamentals.
- Fundamentals skills must become habits.
- Never get away from the basic fundamentals.
- Continue to practice and improve in the fundamentals.
- Keep your focus on the fundamentals that have made us successful.

G

Goals

"Setting a goal is not the main thing. It is deciding how you will go about achieving it and staying with that plan."

> —*Tom Landry, Hall of Fame football coach*

- Goals are the means you use to reach your dreams.
- Create short-term and long-term goals.
- Establish goals that are slightly out of reach but not out of sight.

- Use the acronym SMART—specific, measurable, attainable, realistic, and timely—to establish the criteria for meaningful goal setting.
- Specific goals focus your efforts and define clearly what you are going to do.
- Measurable goals provide concrete criteria so that you can see the changes occur.
- Attainable goals are also called stretch goals because they take a real commitment in order for you to reach them.
- Realistic goals are doable goals based on where you are at the present time.
- Timely goals set a time limit for completion of your goals.
- Make sure you set goals based on what you really want, not what other people expect of you.
- Write down your goals because it keeps your desired end state clear and in focus.
- Always keep your eye on the goal.
- Setting goals without being committed is a sure way to fail.

Gut Feelings

"How you react to changing circumstances is, to some degree, a reflection of the extent of your experiences and how much confidence you have in your gut feelings."

—*Brian Billick, NFL champion coach*

- Trust your gut feelings.
- Gut feelings are the product of your personality, education, and experience.
- When time is critical and your gut feeling tells you to do something, go ahead and do it even when others tell you it's wrong.

H

Habits

"First we form habits, then they form us. Conquer your bad habits, or they'll eventually conquer you."
—*Dr. Rob Gilbert, sport psychologist*

- Sports are games of habit.
- A habit is a conditioned reflex caused by repetitive acts.
- Habits can either be good or bad.
- Game habits are formed in practice.
- If you demonstrate poor habits in practice, you will have poor game habits.
- Once you've formed a habit, it becomes second nature.

Honesty

"You can never be dishonest or lie to a player or try to give him anything less than the squarest deal possible. Try to lie and you lose the team. That means, you say something then turn around and do something else."
—*Paul Brown, Hall of Fame football coach*

- Honesty is the foundation of character.
- You must give honesty to receive it.
- You will lose credibility if you are discovered to be dishonest.
- It is your responsibility to be honest with yourself, teammates, and coaches.
- Make sure your words and actions are one and the same.
- Do not lie, steal, or cheat.

- Be completely honest with yourself.
- Be aware of why you succeed and why you fail.
- Honestly assess your work habits, your attitude, and your commitment.
- Many athletes don't want to hear the truth when it involves them.

Honor

"Success without honor is an unseasoned dish; it will satisfy your hunger, but it won't taste good."

—Joe Paterno, Hall of Fame football coach

- Honor is your integrity.
- Be truthful, honorable, and genuine.
- Do what you say you will do.
- Honor is also the respect that you give to others.
- Show respect to teammates, opponents, coaches, and referees
- Show respect to your sport and appreciate the beauty of the game.

Humility

"The more you lose yourself in something bigger than yourself, the more energy you will have."

—Norman Vincent Peale, author

- Humility comes before honor.
- We first have to humble ourselves before we can become part of a team.

- With humility comes gratitude, which is a key component of great teams.
- It's impossible to be a consistent winner without humility.

Hustle

"Hustle is a talent. It is drive, commitment, persistence, and fire in the belly."

—*Bill Russell, Hall of Fame basketball player*

- Hustle plays are our trademark.
- All loose balls are ours.
- We always make the maximum effort.
- There's no substitute for hustle.
- No opponent will outhustle us.

I

Improvement

"Improvement begins with *I*."

—*Arnold H. Glasow, humorist and author*

- Daily improvement is our goal.
- Never just go through the motions.
- Strive to get better every day.
- Leave the practice field a better player.
- Remember, it's not where you start, it's where you finish that matters.
- Never be satisfied with your knowledge of the game or your skill level.

- The more you improve, the harder you have to work.
- If you want to make the team better, become a better individual player.
- Always remember that as we improve as a team, our opponent is also improving.

Inner Voice

"If you hear a voice within you say 'you cannot paint,' then by all means paint, and that voice will be silenced."
   —*Vincent van Gogh, artist*

- Be aware of the impact that your inner voice has on your performance.
- Productive thinking leads to success.
- Negative thinking results in poor performance.
- Train your mind to delete negative thoughts.
- In moments of doubt, listen to the positive voice inside your head.
- Replace negative thoughts with productive thoughts.
- Worrying about the outcome of the competition instead of your performance leads to poor play.

Integrity

"I look for three things in hiring people. The first is personal integrity, the second is intelligence, and the third is a high energy level. But if you don't have the first, the other two will kill you."
   —*Warren Buffett, business leader*

- Integrity means doing the right thing.
- It takes strength of character to have integrity.
- The most important asset you have as a person is your integrity. Once you lose it, your words carry little weight and your actions become suspect.
- Nothing will turn people against you quicker than to be perceived as dishonest.
- Do whatever it takes to uphold your integrity.
- Always speak the truth.
- When you lie, you create bigger problems for yourself. It makes the problem part of the future.
- Telling the truth is the best problem-solver there is. It makes the problem part of the past.
- Don't distort facts or leave false impressions.
- Don't cover things up.
- If you have integrity, you know what you stand for and you live by the standards you set.
- Be true to your word.
- Your word is your bond.

Intelligence

"Intelligence is quickly seeing things as they are."
—George Santayana, philosopher and poet

- Intelligence gives athletes an edge.
- Play smart.
- See the situation and determine what the circumstance requires.
- Quickly convert rapid analysis into action.

- Be careful not to overanalyze.
- Don't think too much.
- Overanalysis equals paralysis.
- Do not agonize over past results.
- Not trusting yourself results in thinking too much.

Internal Leadership

"On every team, there is a core group that sets the tone for everyone else. If the tone is positive, you have half the battle won. If it is negative, you are beaten before you ever walk on the field."

—*Chuck Noll, Hall of Fame football coach*

Keep the following in mind when you have identified your team leaders and as you look to groom others for the role:

- Internal leadership is vital to team success.
- Team leaders ensure high standards and a strong work ethic.
- Team leaders establish team values.
- Team leaders keep their team from crumbling under pressure.
- Team leaders build unit cohesion.
- Team leaders minimize conflict.
- Team leaders confront team members who violate rules.
- Team leaders are your best insurance against stupidity.
- The best discipline is that which comes from within the team.

J

Jealousy

"Jealousy . . . is a mental cancer."
—B. C. Forbes, financial journalist and author

As the coach, it is up to you to keep an eye out for the signs of jealousy between members of your team. Pay attention to their interactions and how they respond to the success of others.

- Jealousy leads to quarrels, poor morale, and disunity.
- Jealousy within a team creates splinter groups because a jealous player often tries to bring other teammates to his or her side.
- Jealousy may occur when a player is passed over for a starting position or a player on the team receives a lot of accolades and public attention.
- There is no place for jealousy within a team.
- If jealousy persists, a team will never reach its potential.

Journalists

"Four hostile newspapers are more to be feared than a thousand bayonets."
—Napoleon I, military and political leader

- Do not allow your emotions after the game to become headlines in tomorrow's newspaper.
- Be cautious with your remarks to the media.
- The less said the better.
- Always be humble in victory and gracious in defeat.
- Never criticize a teammate to the media.

K

Knowledge

"Our success in some areas could be from something else that we've seen other teams do and copied from them."
    —*Bill Belichick, NFL champion football coach*

- Knowledge is a powerful source of competence and credibility.
- Be a student of the game.
- Always search for new ideas.
- Be committed to continual learning and self-improvement.
- Study the characteristics of players and teams that you want to emulate.
- Learn your strengths and weaknesses.
- Learn the strengths and weaknesses of your teammates.
- Learn the strengths and weaknesses of your opponents.

L

Listen

"If we were supposed to talk more than we listen, we would have two mouths and one ear."
    —*Mark Twain, author*

- The key to learning is listening.
- The ability to listen is a learned skill.
- Listen critically.
- Be an active listener. Look for feelings and attitudes along with the verbal message.

- Listen before you speak.
- Don't compromise your listening skills by thinking about what you're going to say next.
- Don't pretend to understand when you don't.
- Check the accuracy of your listening by paraphrasing.
- Most people are poor listeners.
- Listen carefully when someone you trust speaks.

Losers

"The path of least resistance is the path of the loser."
—H. G. Wells, author

- Losers have no idea what it takes to succeed.
- Losers don't have the work ethic, the desire, or the commitment.
- Losers always have an excuse.
- Losers say it is not their responsibility.
- Losers say it's too difficult.
- Losers are chronic complainers.
- Losers are never satisfied.
- Losers quit.
- There is no place on our team for a loser.

Losing

"Winning is a habit. Unfortunately, so is losing."
—Vince Lombardi, Hall of Fame football coach

- The reality in sport is that one team wins and the other team loses.
- It is essential to determine why a team lost.

- Sometimes a team will play very well and still lose. Other times a team will play poorly and lose.
- Losing elicits powerful emotions.
- How you respond to losing will determine your overall success.
- Losses can be a positive motivator for future success.
- Losses often humble us and shape us into the people we want to be.
- Losses reflect on the performance, not the performer.
- Losses can destroy a team if not dealt with properly.
- Losses bring outside criticism, create doubt, upset team morale, and create dissension within the team.
- Learn everything that you can from the loss and then move on.

Loyalty

"Loyalty means nothing unless it has at its heart the absolute principal of self-sacrifice."
—President Woodrow Wilson

- Loyalty is a two-way street.
- If you want people to be loyal to you, you must be loyal to them.
- Loyalty has a very strong impact on your behavior. It provides the energy to be the best that you can be.
- Be loyal to your personal values.
- Never compromise your integrity.
- Be loyal to our team's core values.
- A team divided against itself can break down at any moment.

Luck

"I'm a great believer in luck, and I find the harder I work, the more I have of it."

—President Thomas Jefferson

- Good fortune and bad fortune occur in life.
- The key is how you respond to events that happen.
- Take advantage of good fortune.
- Take responsibility when faced with bad fortune.
- Don't wallow in self-pity.
- Maintain trust in yourself and your teammates.
- The harder you work, the luckier you get.

M

Mental Performance

"The dividing factor between the team that wins and the one that loses is the mental attitude, the effort they give, and the mental alertness that keeps them from making mental mistakes."

—Tom Seaver, Hall of Fame baseball player

- The difference between a good player and a great one is mostly mental.
- Great players learn how to regulate their mental performance so that it enhances their physical performance.
- Be aware of your thoughts and delete negative messages immediately.

- Establish a routine for disciplining your mind.
- Get rid of distractions.
- Master your self-control and maintain your mental discipline.

Mental Toughness

"Mental toughness is spartanism with qualities of sacrifice, self-denial, dedication. It is fearlessness, and it is love."

—*Vince Lombardi, Hall of Fame football coach*

- Team performance depends on the mental toughness of its athletes.
- Tough-minded athletes last longer than tough times.
- Mental toughness is honesty.
- Mental toughness is courage to face your fears.
- Mental toughness is aggressiveness under control.
- Mental toughness is responsibility.
- Mental toughness is consistency of focus.
- Mental toughness is competitiveness.
- Mental toughness is tenacity.
- Mental toughness is coping effectively with adversity.
- Mental toughness is perseverance.
- Mental toughness is commitment to our team's goals.
- Mental toughness is self-discipline and dedication.
- Mental toughness is responsibility for your behavior.
- Mental toughness is respect for yourself and others.
- Mental toughness can be taught.

Mistakes

"You learn nothing from your successes except to think too much of yourself. It is from failure that all growth comes, provided you can recognize it, admit it, learn from it, rise above it, and then try it again."

—*Dee Hock, business leader*

- Don't be afraid to make mistakes.
- If you're not willing to make mistakes, you're not going to improve.
- Everyone makes mistakes.
- You will never play a perfect game.
- Recover quickly from your mistakes.
- Learn from your mistakes and move on.
- Don't allow mistakes to beat you up.
- Forgive yourself for past mistakes.
- Don't make the same mistake twice.
- Great players study their mistakes and make the needed corrections.

Moments

"To every man there comes in his lifetime that special moment when he is figuratively tapped on the shoulder and offered a chance to do a very special thing, unique to him and fitted to his talents. What a tragedy if that moment finds him unprepared or unqualified for the work which would be his finest hour."

—*Prime Minister Winston Churchill*

- Every goal reaches a moment of execution when it becomes necessary to take action and make the goal a reality.
- Every game has two or three moments that ultimately make the difference between winning and losing.
- Look at each possession as a new day.
- Stay grounded in the moment.
- Focus on what you must do at this moment to excel.
- Make each moment meaningful.

Motivation

"Knowledge alone is not enough to get desired results. You must have the more elusive ability to teach and motivate. This defines a leader; if you can't teach and you can't motivate, you can't lead."

—*John Wooden, Hall of Fame basketball player and coach*

- Motivation is the extra push or drive needed to accomplish a goal.
- Motivation comes from within each of us.
- Motivation is pride, guts, determination, and desire.
- Motivation is based on relationships.

Remember: Players on close-knit teams are highly motivated not to let teammates down. Motivated teams possess a strong desire to succeed.

N

Negativity

"Dwelling on the negative simply contributes to its power."
—*Shirley MacLaine, actress and author*

- Negative players zap the life out of everyone around them.
- Negative attitudes are morale killers.
- People with negative thoughts poison your spirit and well-being.
- Negativity will keep a team from reaching its potential.
- Stay away from negativity and cynicism.
- Negativism is an attitude, and attitudes can be changed.
- Don't dwell on the disappointments and setbacks.

Next Play

"Whatever you have just done is not nearly as important as what you are doing right now."
—*Mike Krzyzewski, Hall of Fame basketball coach*

- The most important play is the next one.
- Don't focus on the last play. It's history.
- Don't waste time worrying about a mistake or celebrating a great play.
- Move on to the next play immediately.

O

Opportunity

"Success is that place in the road where preparation meets opportunity."

—Branch Rickey, Hall of Fame baseball executive

- Every day presents an opportunity to get better and improve.
- Learn to recognize opportunities.
- Create opportunities from setbacks.
- Opportunities are plentiful for those people with positive attitudes.
- There will be more opportunities the harder you work.
- Be ready to make full use of opportunities.
- Treat our successes and failures as opportunities to learn and improve.

Optimism

"In life there are positive and negative thoughts. And hey, it doesn't cost you a cent more to think positively."

—Angelo Dundee, Hall of Fame boxing trainer

- Remain positive and calm in the face of short- and long-term setbacks.
- Be resilient and do not let anything defeat your optimism and positive attitude.

- Program yourself to be optimistic.
- No matter what the situation, find ways to be optimistic.
- Replace pessimism with optimism.
- Negative thoughts during athletic performance are natural, but you must dismiss these thoughts and refocus on the positive.
- A positive and optimistic environment enhances communication, morale, and productivity.
- Have optimism in your voice when you communicate with team members.

Over-Coaching

"Over-coaching can be more harmful than under-coaching."
> —John Wooden, Hall of Fame basketball player
> and coach

Whether you're talking to your assistants or reminding yourself, keep the following in mind as you assess your overall coaching philosophy:

- Keep the game simple.
- Stick to the basics.
- Don't over-coach during games.
- Don't take away all your players' initiative.

Overconfidence

"Overconfident teams are ripe for the picking."
> —Jack Greynolds, Hall of Fame basketball coach

- Confidence is a good thing, but overconfidence sets a team up for failure.
- Don't ever think that you can give less than your best effort and still win.
- Respect all opponents.
- Don't overestimate your ability.
- Never underestimate your opponent.
- Don't look past an opponent.
- Victory is earned as a result of conscientious mental and physical preparation.

P

Passion

"Find something that you love to do and you'll never have to work a day in your life."

—*Harvey MacKay, author*

- Passion is the first step to excellence.
- Passion ignites the fuel that drives us to excel.
- Passion, not talent, takes athletes to the top.
- Passion is what keeps athletes going in the face of adversity and disappointments.
- Passion makes up for a lot of ills.
- Do what you love, and don't let anything stand in your way.
- Passion is contagious.
- Energize yourself by being around positive people.
- Display passion on a daily basis.
- Are you passionate about your sport?

Patience

"Patience and perseverance have a magical effect before which difficulties disappear and obstacles vanish."
—President John Quincy Adams

- Patience is a powerful virtue.
- Patient athletes let their performance flow rather than trying too hard to make it happen.
- Remain calm and don't rush your performance.
- If you are a backup player, prepare for success as you wait for your opportunity.
- Realize that good things take time.
- Look at the season as a marathon rather than a sprint.

Pay the Price

"If everyone doesn't pay the price to win, then everyone will pay the price by losing."
—John C. Maxwell, author

- To achieve any level of success requires every one of us to pay the price.
- Once we reach a level of success, then we must all pay an even greater price to stay there.

Perfectionism

"Striving for excellence motivates you. Striving for perfection is demoralizing."
—Harriet B. Braiker, psychologist and author

- You will never play a perfect game.
- Stop being so hard on yourself.
- Don't beat yourself up for not being perfect.
- Look at all the things that you do to help the team rather than focusing on your mistakes.

Perseverance

"In the realm of ideas, everything depends on enthusiasm; in the real world, all rests on perseverance."

—Johann Wolfgang von Goethe, author and theorist

- Athletics is one of the best venues to teach people how to persevere through difficult times.
- Without the will to persevere, all the skill in the world won't make you a winner.
- Always finish what you start.
- Get back up and keep going stronger than ever after you have gotten knocked down.

Persistence

"Nothing in the world can take the place of persistence. Talent will not; nothing is more common than unsuccessful men with talent. Genius will not; unrewarded genius is almost a proverb. Education will not; the world is full of educated derelicts. Persistence and determination alone are omnipotent."

—President Calvin Coolidge

- Never quit.
- Play hard every minute, every second, of every game.

- Outstanding athletes deliver their best possible performance even though they may be having a bad day.
- Learn how to maintain your focus and concentration even when things are not going well. Winning ugly is an attribute of successful athletes.

Planning

"A good plan is like a road map: it shows the final destination and usually the best way to get there."
—*H. Stanley Judd, author*

- Proper planning prevents poor performance.
- In order to be prepared, it is essential that you create an action plan.
- Always have a contingency plan and an emergency plan.

Playing Time

"They said you have to use your five best players but I found you win with the five who fit together the best."
—*Red Auerbach, Hall of Fame basketball coach*

- Playing time is a reward.
- You earn playing time by your play in practice.
- Never take your playing time for granted.

Poise

"The key to winning is poise under stress."
—*Paul Brown, Hall of Fame football coach*

- Maintain focus on what needs to be done.
- Stay calm, cool, and collected.
- Concentrate on what you can control.
- Go out there and do your job.
- Clutch performers possess the ability to keep their poise when those around them are losing theirs.
- Maintain an internal balance when surrounded by chaos.
- Poise makes you appear stronger in the eyes of your opponents.
- Never allow your opponent or hostile crowds to see that you are rattled.
- Championship teams demonstrate team poise. They exhibit confidence and poise when the game is on the line.

Practice

"You can't make a great play unless you do it first in practice."
—*Chuck Noll, Hall of Fame football coach*

- Our practices are as gamelike as possible.
- The purpose of practice is to improve in all areas of the game.
- Practice is where habits are formed and relationships are built.
- Practice the right way every day.
- The quality of your practice habits indicates whether you are truly committed.
- Practice with the same mental concentration called for in a game.
- Practice the same way that you want to perform in a game.

- Develop good habits through proper preparation in practice.
- Perfect practice makes perfect.
- Practice makes permanent.
- The game may be played on Saturday, but it is won on the practice field during the week.
- Practice every day so you can beat the best.

Praise

"You can accomplish anything in life provided you don't mind who gets the credit."
—*President Harry S. Truman*

- Give credit to others.
- Acknowledge teammates for their part in team success.
- We place the team above individual accomplishments, but we will do everything that we can to promote individual accomplishments.
- When you do something that improves our team, we will make sure that everyone within our organization knows it.

Preparation

"Winning is the science of being totally prepared."
—*George Allen, Hall of Fame football coach*

- Preparation is the foundation for success.
- Preparation precedes excellence.
- Preparation promotes a positive outlook.
- The will to win is meaningless without the will to prepare.
- A winning effort begins with preparation.

- There is a very thin line that separates greatness from mediocrity and success from failure. The will to prepare makes the difference.
- The best way to combat stress is to be prepared.
- There are no shortcuts to success.
- If you fail to prepare, you prepare to fail.
- Be prepared for your opportunity.
- The more prepared you are, the less chance you have of getting distracted.
- Being prepared requires commitment, perspective, and action.
- Preparation requires mental and physical conditioning.
- Being totally prepared incorporates the acronym PACE. There is a primary plan, an alternate plan, a contingency plan, and an emergency plan.

Pressure

"What this game is all about is whether or not you can execute under pressure in critical situations."

—Bill Belichick, NFL champion football coach

- Great athletes learn how to deal with pressure, thrive on it, and make it their own.
- We have been taught to think of pressure as the enemy.
- Prepare for pressure situations.
- Embrace pressure and use it to your advantage.
- Look at pressure as an opportunity to show how good you are.
- If you can control pressure, you can make it work for you rather than against you.

- Don't use pressure as an excuse.
- Never back down from pressure situations.
- Thrive on pressure.
- Pressure is built into athletics. Your responsibility is to relieve excess tension.
- Be intense, not tense.

Pride

"Show class, have pride, and demonstrate character. If you do, winning takes care of itself."

—Paul "Bear" Bryant, Hall of Fame football coach

- Pride is the result of being and doing your best.
- Pride is self-respect.
- Take pride in your behavior, your accomplishments, and the actions of your teammates.
- Take pride in daily improvement.
- Team pride comes from a group of players who place team goals above their own personal achievement.
- You must demonstrate pride in our team and always get the most out of your ability, regardless of the time it takes.
- Always remember that pain is temporary. Pride is forever.
- Our team will play hard and demonstrate pride at all times.
- There is a bonding, a team pride that develops among players on a winning team.
- Take pride in the things that will make us great.
- Pride is not arrogance or a sense of entitlement.
- Don't let pride get in the way of doing the right thing.

Procrastination

"Procrastination is the fear of success. Because success is heavy, it carries a responsibility with it. It is much easier to procrastinate and live on the 'someday-I'll' philosophy."
—Denis Waitley, author

- Confront hard work and responsibility.
- Recognize those things that are important and get them done.
- Develop a daily routine so that you are not putting things off.
- Start early on projects.
- Take responsibility for getting things done on time.

Punctuality

"Punctuality at practice should not be compromised."
—Bob Knight, Hall of Fame basketball coach

- Arrive early or on time.
- If you are one minute late, you're being disrespectful to each of your teammates and coaches.
- Tardiness is a lack of self-discipline.
- Plan accordingly so that you are not late.

Purpose

"A man without a purpose is like a ship without a rudder."
—Thomas Carlyle, author

- Know what you want and where you are going.
- Live with purpose.
- Fulfilling our purpose is part of who we are.

Q

Quitting

"Once you learn to quit, it becomes a habit."

—Vince Lombardi, Hall of Fame football coach

- The bottom line is that we never quit.
- Don't ever give up or stop playing.
- If you quit on yourself, you have nothing left.
- No player wants to be known as a quitter.
- Quitting is not an option.
- The scoreboard may indicate that we ran out of time before victory prevailed, but we will never quit.

R

Reality

"The first responsibility of a leader is to define reality."

—Max DePree, business leader

As the coach, you have the vantage point of being able to see the big picture first, in terms of strengths, weaknesses, and potential problems. You will define the reality of your team's situation for your players, but you must also deal with it:

- Confront reality.
- Directly address issues before they turn into major problems.
- Don't withhold bad news.
- Don't bury your head in the sand.

Relationships

"Most of the difficulties facing our young people have been caused by a breakdown of important one-to-one relationships."
—Tom Osborne, Hall of Fame football coach

- Relationships are built on respect and trust.
- When a team has strong relationships among its players, it can weather any internal storm.

Repetition

"We are what we repeatedly do. Excellence then, is not an act, it is a habit."
—Aristotle, philosopher

- Successful preparation depends on maximizing meaningful repetitions.
- Think of the term REPS as an acronym meaning "repetition elevates personal skills."
- Repetition is not fun, but it makes strong teams.
- You will get what you emphasize.

Resilience

"A successful man is one who can lay a firm foundation with the bricks others have thrown at him."

—David Brinkley, television journalist

- Always bounce back from failure.
- Be stronger because of your losses and disappointments.
- Never let anything break your spirit.
- Stay tough during difficult times.
- Never lose belief in yourself and your teammates.

Respect

"I've learned that the only way to get respect from people is to give them respect."

—Tommy Lasorda, Hall of Fame baseball manager

- Respect the dignity of every person.
- Treat everyone with respect, especially those who can't do anything for you.
- Respect is essential to building team unity.
- Players who do not respect others will not make good teammates.
- You don't have to like each other, but you do have to respect one another as teammates.
- Treat teammates the way that you would like to be treated.
- You earn respect from others through your actions.
- Be professional.

Responsibilities of a Coach

"Good coaching may be defined as the development of character, personality and habits of players, plus the teaching of fundamentals and team play."

—*Clair Bee, Hall of Fame basketball coach*

Much of this book relates to what you expect from the athletes you lead. To be worthy of their response, keep these responsibilities in mind, and instill them in your staff as well:

- Provide a wholesome environment in which players can develop physically, mentally, emotionally, socially, and spiritually.
- Create an educational setting based on values in which players learn life lessons and improve their quality of life.
- Teach players how to become athletes of character.
- Promote fair play and sportsmanship.
- Teach the importance of being a good team member.
- Create an environment that is rewarding and fun for athletes.
- Never place winning ahead of a team member.
- Be the type of coach that we would want our son or daughter to play for.

Responsibilities of a Player

"Great teams have players who understand their responsibilities."

—*Bruce Brown, coach and author*

- Many players want the prestige and status of being on a team, but they don't want the responsibility and commitment that go along with it.
- It is a privilege to be a member of this team.
- Always speak the truth.
- Play hard.
- Be respectful.
- Have a positive attitude.
- Be eager to learn and improve every day.
- Make no excuses.
- Compliment teammates.
- Do everything within your power never to let a fellow teammate down.
- Become the best team member that you can be.

Responsibility

"The price of greatness is responsibility."
　　　　—Prime Minister Winston Churchill

- You are personally responsible for everything that you think and do.
- Accept full responsibility for your actions.
- We will clearly define your responsibilities.
- Take responsibility for results.
- With tradition comes responsibility.

Results

"Leadership is defined by results not attributes."
　　　　—Peter F. Drucker, business strategist and author

- Now is the time to make it happen.
- Get things done.
- We want visible and tangible results.
- The key is productivity.
- Results help create a winning culture.
- Results inspire others.
- Basically, we are divided into three groups. Those people who make things happen, those who watch things happen, and those who wonder what happened.
- Always remember that the world doesn't care about your self-esteem. It expects results first and foremost.
- Are you working hard and getting things accomplished?

Risk

"To win without risk is to triumph without glory."
—Pierre Corneille, playwright

- You must have the courage to take risks.
- People who are afraid to take risks will not grow.
- The key is to take intelligent risks.

Roles

"Sometimes a player's greatest challenge is coming to grips with his role on the team."
—Scottie Pippen, NBA All-Star player

- On a team, everyone makes a difference.
- Recognize that your role is important to the success of our team.

- Each player makes his or her unique contribution to the team's success.
- Everyone must do his or her job, no matter how big or small, in order for the team to be successful.
- It is essential that you not only accept your role, but that you excel in it.
- You will flourish in your role as a team player as long as you put your whole self into the tasks that you have been given.
- Players must understand that the team goal is more important than their individual roles.
- In order to build teamwork, all team members must feel useful and understand their role in the success of our team.
- Every successful team has role players.

Rules

"Too many rules get in the way of leadership."
—Mike Krzyzewski, Hall of Fame basketball coach

- Rules are designed to achieve team cohesion and mutual respect.
- Don't do anything that is detrimental to yourself or this team.
- Never lie, steal, or cheat.
- Treat all team members with respect.
- Always be on time.
- Play hard, play smart, and play together.
- Have a positive attitude and always put the team first.

S

Sacrifice

"If a team is to reach its potential, each player must be willing to subordinate his personal goals to the good of the team."

—*Bud Wilkinson, Hall of Fame football coach*

- Dedication to a sport requires sacrifices.
- To be a great player will take hours and hours of practice.
- Without sacrifice, you will never know your own potential.
- Every player must be willing to make sacrifices for our team to succeed.
- Always put the team first.

Self-Control

"The cyclone derives its power from a calm center. So does a person."

—*Norman Vincent Peale, author*

- Learn how to control your impulses, emotions, and desires.
- Self-control influences your ability to act properly regardless of the circumstances.
- Self-control is refraining from profanity and vulgar language.
- Self-control is refraining from arguments with referees and opponents.
- Self-control is refraining from temper outbursts or displaying anger after a mistake, loss, or poor performance.
- Self-control is refraining from trash-talking.

- Self-control is refraining from over-celebrating and gamesmanship tactics.
- If you lack self-control, you will never be able to earn confidence from your teammates and coaches.

Self-Discipline

"Discipline yourself, and others won't need to."

—*John Wooden, Hall of Fame basketball player and coach*

- Self-discipline is the internal mechanism that drives you to do what is needed in order to be successful.
- You will never be able to reach your potential without self-discipline.
- Laziness is not always about a lack of desire; it is about the lack of self-discipline.
- If you are not disciplined, you will never be able to lead by example.
- Eliminate any tendency to make excuses.
- Without self-discipline, our team has little chance of winning.
- Self-disciplined players have a positive effect on everyone around them.

Self-Esteem

"Outstanding leaders go out of their way to boost the self-esteem of their personnel. If people believe in themselves, it's amazing what they can accomplish."

—*Sam Walton, business leader*

- Your self-esteem is the most important factor in reaching your potential.
- Players with low self-esteem underachieve.
- You will never experience greatness unless you feel good about yourself.
- You must believe that you are an important member of this team.
- You must believe that you are essential to our team's accomplishments.
- You must believe that you deserve success.
- Don't derive your self-esteem from material objects.

Self-Fulfilling Prophecy

"If a coach tells his football team that it is no good, it is often not long before the team fulfills that prophecy by becoming worse."
—Tom Osborne, Hall of Fame football coach

- We tend to get what we expect, both from ourselves and from others.
- When we expect more, we get more.
- When we expect less, we get less.
- A player predicting failure will fail.
- Thinking about what you don't want to happen greatly increases the chance that it will happen.
- Having a mind-set of expecting to win increases the odds of winning.

Self-Image

"Your self-image should not come from the job you do but how
well you do your job."
—Martin Luther King Jr., pastor and civil-rights leader

- Your self-image is basically the total sum of all your beliefs
  about yourself.
- Your self-image is your blueprint for success.
- Your performance is a direct reflection of the image that
  you have of yourself.
- A poor self-image places artificial limitations on you.
- Replace your negative beliefs with positive ones.
- There is no opinion as important to your overall success as
  the opinion you have of yourself.
- You control the key to your self-image.

Self-Talk

"Affirmations and positive self-talk can help athletes focus on
their strengths rather than their weaknesses."
—Ralph Vernacchia, sports psychologist and author

- Self-talk is critical to enhanced performance.
- Change your self-talk so that it focuses on what you want
  to do.
- Listen to the positive voice inside of you.
- Positive self-talk helps focus in the present.
- Positive self-talk maintains concentration.
- Positive self-talk avoids dwelling on past mistakes.
- We must continually work to improve our self-talk.

Self-Trust

"Self-trust is the first secret of success . . . the essence of heroism."
—*Ralph Waldo Emerson, philosopher and poet*

- Believe in yourself.
- Trust the results.
- Abundant self-trust builds self-confidence.
- If you don't trust your abilities during competition, your performance will be subpar.
- Lack of self-trust weakens your ability to trust others.

Selfishness

"Great achievement is usually born of great sacrifice, and is never the result of selfishness."
—*Napoleon Hill, author*

- Eliminate "me first" thinking.
- Never put yourself ahead of the team.
- Selfish players develop an overpowering belief in their own importance.
- Selfishness impedes success.
- When selfishness is tolerated, the entire team is in jeopardy.
- There are many teams that have great talent and can't win because of the selfishness of their players.

Selfless Service

"A person really does not become whole until he or she becomes a part of something that's bigger than himself or herself."
—*Jim Valvano, NCAA champion basketball coach*

- Selfless service is a genuine willingness to put the team above one's own interests.
- Selfless service doesn't mean that you can't have high ambition and personal goals.
- Selfless service does mean that you have to be willing to sacrifice for the greater good of the team.

Setbacks

"Anytime you suffer a setback or disappointment, put your head down and plow ahead."
　　　　—Les Brown, author

- Don't allow setbacks to become permanent obstacles.
- Quickly regroup after a setback and prepare for the next challenge.
- Self-confidence helps one overcome setbacks.
- Don't take setbacks personally.
- You must believe in yourself and your teammates during setbacks and disappointments.

Shortcuts

"There's no shortcut to building a team each season. You build the foundation brick by brick."
　　　　—Bill Belichick, NFL champion coach

- There are no shortcuts to success.
- You can't skip steps when building a championship team.
- Success requires thorough planning and skillful execution.

Simplicity

"Keep it simple—when you get too complex you forget the obvious."

—Al McGuire, Hall of Fame basketball coach

- Keep it simple.
- Many times, less is more.
- Do not make the game more complicated than it is.
- Don't allow your life to become too complicated.

Step by Step

"Inch by inch, life's a cinch. Yard by yard, it's really hard."

—Morgan Wootten, Hall of Fame basketball coach

- You will reach your goals one step at a time, one day at a time, and with the understanding that it will take many steps and many days to ensure that you get there.
- Focus on one game at a time, one practice at a time, and one play at a time.
- Focus on making a positive play rather than a big play.
- Go for the single rather than the home run.
- Before you can realize your dream, you have to deal with the reality of your situation and change it one step at a time.

Strengths

"You really have to look inside yourself and find your own inner strength, and say, I'm proud of what I am and who I am, and I'm just going to be myself."

—Mariah Carey, singer

- We all have strengths that once put into action will propel us past our expectations.
- Discover your strengths, and you have found the switch for success.
- Maximize your strengths.
- Place yourself in position to allow your strengths to shine.
- Make the most of what you have and don't worry about what you lack.
- To make the team better, find ways to use your strengths within the framework of the team.

Success

"Success is peace of mind which is a direct result of self-satisfaction in knowing that you did your best to become the best you are capable of becoming."

—*John Wooden, Hall of Fame basketball player and coach*

- Success is an everyday proposition.
- Success comes from doing the little things right day after day.
- The crucial elements for success are commitment, desire, outlook, and responsibility.
- Success must be earned.
- Success is not measured by heights attained but by obstacles overcome.
- Team success should be your daily focus.
- Focus on realizing your full potential so that your team is successful.

- Concentrate on being the best that you can be as an individual and a team member.
- The shelf life of success can be very limited.
- It is surprising how many people do not know how to deal with success.
- Never forget what it took to get you to the top.
- Don't abandon the things that got you there.
- Maintain the self-discipline that is necessary to be the best.
- The minute you start believing that you accomplished something alone, you will be alone.
- Remind yourself that your success has come from within, not from the expectations of others.
- Maintaining success is as important as achieving it.

Support System

"No matter how involved you are in what you do, no matter how many hours a week you devote to your career pursuits, you must always remember that your family is your primary team."

—Mike Krzyzewski, Hall of Fame basketball coach

- Take time to be with family and friends.
- Develop a positive support system.
- Surround yourself with positive people.
- Shrink your social circle to those people you trust.
- Associate with people who will keep you from getting too high or too low.
- Share your success with people who helped you achieve it.

T

Talent

"Hard work without talent is a shame, but talent without hard
   work is a tragedy."
>   —*Robert Half, business leader*

- Talent has to be developed.
- Recognize your talents and use them to benefit the team.
- How can you better maximize the talents that you have?
- What talents might you have that have not been developed
  yet?
- Championship teams do not always have the most talented
  individuals.
- There are many highly talented athletes who never win
  championships.
- Talented players who aren't willing to sacrifice for the
  greater good of the team destroy team chemistry.
- No collection of players, no matter how talented, can win
  unless they form a team.

Team

"Success is the inner satisfaction and peace of mind that come
   from knowing I did the best I was capable of doing for the
   group."
>   —*Jim Tressel, NCAA champion football coach*

It is up to the coach to define the team for his players as a concept greater than a group in matching uniforms:

- A team has a clearly defined and shared sense of purpose.
- A team shares a value system.
- A team has players who are united by a shared goal.
- A team has players who bond tightly and understand that they need each other in order to be the best.
- A team exhibits positive peer pressure to optimize collective performance.
- A team's players maintain their attitude, work ethic, and togetherness even when they are losing and trying to turn it around.
- A team never quits no matter what the situation.
- The word TEAM is an acronym for "together everyone achieves more."

Team Captains

"All it takes is one person who is committed, focused, and on a mission to spark an entire team into believing in themselves."
—*Bruce Brown, coach and author*

Your team captains have earned a position of leadership from their peers. It's up to you to remind them of the responsibilities that go along with it:

- Effective team captains are positive and enthusiastic.
- Effective team captains are trustworthy.
- Effective team captains are the hardest workers at practice.
- Effective team captains are responsible.
- Effective team captains model mental toughness.
- Effective team captains are steady under pressure.

- Effective team captains are focused on the team's core values and goals.
- Effective team captains always place the team first.
- Effective team captains challenge teammates.
- Effective team captains are good listeners.
- Effective team captains are humble.
- Effective team captains are decisive.
- Effective team captains have the courage to face problems.
- Effective team captains are positive role models.
- Effective team captains represent themselves and their team with class and pride.

Team Ego

"My ego always was a team ego. It was totally linked with the success of my team. It wasn't linked to personal achievement."
—*Bill Russell, Hall of Fame basketball player*

- Individual egos can poison a team.
- Transfer your individual ego into a team ego.
- Players today don't have a strong sense of team ego.
- Place team success ahead of personal success.
- We will become a great team when every player establishes a team ego.
- Are you willing to lower your individual goals and make personal sacrifices for the good of the team?

Teamwork

"Teamwork is really a form of trust. It's what happens when you surrender the mistaken idea that you can go it alone and realize that you won't achieve your individual goals without the support of your colleagues."

—*Pat Summitt, Hall of Fame basketball coach*

- No team will succeed without teamwork, no matter how many All-Americans it has.
- Teamwork is individual commitment to a team effort.
- Teamwork requires that every player be on the same page.
- In order for teamwork to take place, all players must function as a cohesive unit, not just a collection of individuals.
- No one succeeds alone.
- The essence of teamwork is selfless service.
- The greatest threat to our team is not our opponent but dissension from within the ranks.
- Teamwork elevates everyone's play.
- Teamwork comes from mutual respect and internal leadership.
- Great teams are defined by their teamwork.
- Teamwork separates winners and losers.

Traditions

"Traditions help shape and reflect the character of your team—
past, present, and future. Traditions refocus you and give you
perspective, rekindle the spirit of the past, remind you of what is
important, and create a link that binds the past to the present."
—Bruce Brown, coach and author

- The faces may change, the uniforms may be different, but tradition never graduates.
- Traditions motivate players to an established standard of excellence.
- Traditions help sustain a program's success.
- The past successes of our program are very important.
- Respect the players who walked this path before you.

Trust

"Whether you're on a sports team, in an office, or a member of a
family, if you can't trust one another there's going to be trouble."
—Joe Paterno, Hall of Fame football coach

- Trust is belief in your team and teammates.
- Trust holds a team together.
- Trust is the key to teamwork.
- Without truth, there can be no trust.
- Without trust, there can be no relationships.
- Without relationships, there can be no long-term success.
- For a team to succeed, every individual must have a trusting relationship with every other member of the team.
- It is amazing what can be accomplished when teammates trust one another.

- Trust, but also verify.
- Don't extend your trust to everyone.
- Always trust with your eyes open.

U

Unity

"Every team requires unity. A team has to move as one unit, one force, with each person understanding and assisting the roles of his teammates. If your team doesn't do this, whatever the reason, it goes down in defeat. You win or lose as a team, as a family."

—*Jack Kemp, NFL player, politician, and author*

- There is nothing greater than being a member of a close-knit team working toward a shared dream.
- We must build a high level of trust, respect, and commitment so that our team can withstand the inevitable conflicts and tensions that occur throughout the season.
- Straight communication is an important key to team unity.
- Cooperate with one another in order to build a sense of collective faith.
- Disagreements and tension must not affect a team's unity.
- Develop an "all for one and one for all" mind-set.
- One team, one fight.
- Winning is tough enough when we are all pulling together. When we are pulling in different directions, we have no chance.
- Develop unit cohesion.
- Stick together as a team win or lose.

Unselfishness

"The individual that lives only for himself finally reaps nothing but unhappiness. Selfishness corrodes. Unselfishness ennobles, satisfies. Don't put off the joy derivable from doing helpful, kindly things for others."
>   —*B. C. Forbes, business leader*

- The aim of everything that we are doing is to forgo individual credit for the good of our team, because if the team benefits, the individual will benefit.
- True success is achieved when one's primary focus is on the team.
- Great teams have unselfish players.
- Unselfish players are able to accomplish extraordinary things.
- Are you more concerned about yourself or the welfare of this team?

V

Values

"Shared values define a team."
>   —*John C. Maxwell, author*

- Values provide a solid foundation that keeps everyone together.
- Values provide a moral compass for doing what is right.
- Our team has established values.
- Our values are defined in behavioral expectations.
- We teach and practice our values in everything that we do.

- Our values are not just words.
- Our actions align with our values.
- Our values become our team's identity.
- Are you clear on our team's values?

Vision

"It is a terrible thing to see and have no vision."

—Helen Keller, author

- The first step in becoming great is to envision what it is that you want.
- Your vision is what you will become.
- For true greatness to occur, all players must be united and committed to our vision.
- To reach our vision requires all players to stretch their expectations, aspirations, and performances.
- We will put our vision in writing so that it can serve as a constant reminder to our team.
- Vision statements are not wishful thinking. They are based on the reality of our resources and talent.
- Our vision fuels our commitment to do whatever it takes to achieve excellence.
- Vision permits us to convert dreams into the reality of success through hard work.
- Always see the big picture and never lose the passion of your dreams.

Successful coaches are able to create a vision, identify steps to reach that vision, and assess the progress of the team in accomplishing that vision.

Vitality

"Vitality shows not only in the ability to persist but the ability to start over."

—F. Scott Fitzgerald, author

- A team's identity comes from its vitality.
- Vitality is mental toughness.
- Vitality is physical strength.
- Vitality is the power of enduring.
- Vitality is growing and developing.
- Vitality is energy.

W

Weaknesses

"Do not let what you cannot do interfere with what you can do."

—John Wooden, Hall of Fame basketball player and coach

- Identify your weaknesses.
- Minimize your weaknesses.
- Build up your weaknesses so they become assets to the team.

Whiners

"I can't stand it when a player whines. A winner never whines."

—Paul Brown, Hall of Fame football coach

- Don't fall into the trap of self-pity, finger-pointing, and whining.
- Stop complaining.

- It's not all about you.
- There is no place on our team for whiners.
- Get over it and move on.
- Focus on the team, not yourself.

Will

"The difference between a successful person and others is not a lack of strength, not a lack of knowledge, but rather in a lack of will."

—Vince Lombardi, Hall of Fame football coach

- Everyone wants to succeed, but not everyone has the will to do what it takes to succeed.
- The will to win is self-discipline.
- The will to win is desire.
- The will to win is determination.
- The will to win is commitment.
- The will to win is mental toughness.
- The will to win is never giving up.
- Wanting something without having the will to win achieves nothing.

Winners

"The man who wins may have been counted out several times, but he didn't hear the referee."

—H. E. Jansen, author

- Winners have mental toughness and discipline.
- Winners think and act positively.
- Winners confront adversity rather than running away.

- Winners recognize that adversity is part of sport and do not magnify the adverse situation.
- Winners know their limitations rather than trying to do more than they are capable of.
- Winners exhibit drive, competitiveness, determination, and commitment.
- Winners see opportunities where others see defeat.
- Winners make every possible effort, all the time, to win.
- Winners recognize their mistakes and learn from them.
- Winners are always trying to get better.
- Winners treat teammates the way they themselves want to be treated.
- Winners hold themselves accountable for their actions.
- Winners come to practice prepared rather than just showing up.
- Winners arrive early rather than just on time or late.

Winning

"I don't think you necessarily have victory when you outscore someone, and I don't think you are necessarily defeated when you're outscored."

—John Wooden, Hall of Fame basketball player and coach

- Success and winning are not one and the same.
- Focus on excellence, not winning.
- Winning is the result of preparation, dedication, desire, attitude, execution, teamwork, and talent.
- Winning is determined by team play.
- Knowing how to win is essential.

- We must eliminate the reasons for losing.
- The will to prepare to win is critical.
- Players must play to win rather than playing not to lose.
- Winning breeds winning. The more you do it, the more you believe that you can do it.
- Every win helps get the next one.
- Understand and believe that we deserve to win.
- There will be a game in which we do not play our best, but that is no excuse for losing.
- To be a consistent winner, you must learn how to perform effectively when you're tired or not feeling well.
- Overemphasis on winning can be a real negative if you use it to judge yourself as an individual and as a team.

Winning and Losing

"Winning coaches should always remember that there is only a one-foot difference between a halo and a noose."
—Bobby Bowden, Hall of Fame football coach

- The line between winning and losing can be a fine one.
- Games are often decided by a matter of inches.
- Proper preparation, execution, and poise are keys to winning close games.
- Championship teams possess the ability to win the close games.

Work

"There is no substitute for work. It is the price of success."
—Earl "Red" Blaik, Hall of Fame football coach

- All great teams have one common denominator, and that is a second-to-none work ethic.
- The difference between good and great is extra effort.
- Nothing meaningful comes without working hard.
- We deserve victory because our team is the hardest-working team in America.
- We won't be outworked.
- Go the extra mile.
- Hard work and togetherness will take us to the top.
- When our most talented players are also our hardest workers, we've got a great chance for real success.
- Work with passion.
- Never allow your work ethic to fall out of the band of excellence.
- The harder you work, the harder it is to give up.
- Athletes who work only as much as is required always underachieve.
- Hard work is hard work, but the results of hard work are fun and rewarding.

Work Smart

"Don't mistake activity for production."
—John Wooden, Hall of Fame basketball player and coach

- Putting in long hours and working extraordinarily hard do not necessarily mean that you will succeed.
- Establish a simple and effective blueprint for success.
- Always look at what you want to accomplish and decide on the best way of doing it.

- Don't waste time or energy on things that aren't important.
- Be realistic. Do not underestimate the demands on your time.
- Prioritize. Clearly establish those things that must be done first.
- Don't waste time.
- Create time in your schedule to get revitalized.
- Never underestimate the importance of rest and recovery.
- Delegate and have confidence in your assistants.

X

X's and O's

"A common mistake among those who work in sport is spending a disproportional amount of time on X's and O's as compared to time spent learning about people."

—Mike Krzyzewski, Hall of Fame basketball coach

- X's and O's are the analytic part of the game and are very important.
- Players must be positioned in the right place at the right time to maximize a team's strengths.
- But even more important than the X's and O's are the people involved.
- Teams win with good people.
- Teams win with execution.
- Great coaches teach fundamentals and motivate and inspire their players.
- Great coaches teach athletes how to play the game rather than teaching specific offenses and defenses.

Y

"Yes, but . . ." Athletes

"The yes-but response is an indication that the person will not get the message. The athlete is focused on what he wants to say, in order to preempt what he doesn't want to hear."

—H. A. Dorfman, sport psychologist and author

- When receiving constructive criticism, a champion doesn't use the phrase "Yes, but . . . ."
- Using the phrase "Yes, but . . ." indicates that you are unwilling to seek a strategy to get better.
- "Yes, but . . ." inhibits learning and performance.

Z

Zeal

"Zeal will do more than knowledge."

—William Hazlitt, author

- Zeal fuels a winning spirit that never gives in.
- Champions demonstrate their zeal through enthusiasm, vitality, passion, spirit, and energy.
- Unrestrained zeal negatively affects performance.
- Be enthusiastic and passionate, but always remain under control.

About the Author

Dr. Ralph Pim is the director of competitive sports in the Department of Physical Education at the United States Military Academy and oversees a program that has more than 3,300 cadet-athletes participating in 24 competitive club sports and 12 company athletics sports. In 2008, West Point was recognized as one of the 15 Most Influential Sport Education Teams in America by the Institute for International Sport.

During Pim's tenure, West Point implemented the Champions of Character program, established both the Mike Krzyzewski Teaching Character Through Sport Award and the General Hal Moore Warrior of Excellence Award, and introduced the Character in Sports Grading Index. Since 2005, West Point has won 27 competitive club national championships.

Pim has earned an excellent reputation as an outstanding teacher and team builder. Prior to his arrival at West Point, he coached basketball for more than 25 years. He coached at Barberton (Ohio) High School, Northwestern State University, Central Michigan University, Alma College, the College of William and Mary, and Limestone College. In 2007, he was inducted into the Limestone College Athletics Hall of Fame.

Pim has authored or coauthored eight books and is a frequent speaker at national conferences on character development through sport. He was one of 12 individuals selected by the Institute for International Sport and The Positive Coaching Alliance at Stanford University as the 2009 Sports Ethics Fellows. Pim is a graduate of Springfield College. He earned his master's degree from Ohio State University and his doctorate from Northwestern State University. He is a member of the Phi Kappa Phi honor society.

The Right Phrase for
Every Situation...Every Time

Perfect Phrases for Building Strong Teams
Perfect Phrases for Business Letters
Perfect Phrases for Business Proposals and Business Plans
Perfect Phrases for Business School Acceptance
Perfect Phrases for College Application Essays
Perfect Phrases for Cover Letters
Perfect Phrases for Customer Service
Perfect Phrases for Dealing with Difficult People
Perfect Phrases for Dealing with Difficult Situations at Work
Perfect Phrases for Documenting Employee Performance Problems
Perfect Phrases for Executive Presentations
Perfect Phrases for Landlords and Property Managers
Perfect Phrases for Law School Acceptance
Perfect Phrases for Lead Generation
Perfect Phrases for Managers and Supervisors
Perfect Phrases for Managing Your Small Business
Perfect Phrases for Medical School Acceptance
Perfect Phrases for Meetings
Perfect Phrases for Motivating and Rewarding Employees
Perfect Phrases for Negotiating Salary & Job Offers
Perfect Phrases for Perfect Hiring
Perfect Phrases for the Perfect Interview
Perfect Phrases for Performance Reviews
Perfect Phrases for Real Estate Agents & Brokers
Perfect Phrases for Resumes
Perfect Phrases for Sales and Marketing Copy
Perfect Phrases for the Sales Call
Perfect Phrases for Setting Performance Goals
Perfect Phrases for Small Business Owners
Perfect Phrases for the TOEFL Speaking and Writing Sections
Perfect Phrases for Writing Grant Proposals
Perfect Phrases in American Sign Language for Beginners
Perfect Phrases in French for Confident Travel
Perfect Phrases in German for Confident Travel
Perfect Phrases in Italian for Confident Travel
Perfect Phrases in Spanish for Confident Travel to Mexico
Perfect Phrases in Spanish for Construction
Perfect Phrases in Spanish for Gardening and Landscaping
Perfect Phrases in Spanish for Household Maintenance and Child Care
Perfect Phrases in Spanish for Restaurant and Hotel Industries

Visit mhprofessional.com/perfectphrases for a complete product listing.

Learn more. Do more.